MURDER & MAYHEM
IN
NORTON, OHIO

LISA ANN MERRICK

THE
History
PRESS

Published by The History Press
Charleston, SC
www.historypress.com

First published 2021

ISBN 9781540248299

Library of Congress Control Number: 2021934594

Notice: The information in this book is true and complete to the best of our knowledge. It is offered without guarantee on the part of the author or The History Press. The author and The History Press disclaim all liability in connection with the use of this book.

To all of the Norton citizens past and present who have been injured, killed or impacted somehow in the following stories, it is an honor to keep your memories alive and sadly for some a tragic reminder of yesterday.

CONTENTS

ACKNOWLEDGEMENTS

F irst, I would like to thank everyone who helped me accomplish this personal goal of publishing my second book during the ongoing coronavirus pandemic. The virus made it exceptionally challenging to obtain materials either through email or phone calls or in person communication. I had to rely heavily on the *Akron Beacon Journal* for most of my information.

Jane Ann Turzillo, fellow author who has published through Arcadia and The History Press, was always available for questions small and large. Thanks for your assistance and your encouragement.

To Jerry Irby, thanks for your help on the Baltic/Deibel tales and to Janean Skiles Ray for computer assistance when my mastery of all things computer seemed dire.

To Patricia Snyder, curator for the Biery House and Museum, thanks for your support in this endeavor even though the topic is not your cup of tea. To Rodger Ramsthaler I give a nod for answering as many questions as I could come up with about the Norton area when all seemed futile.

INTRODUCTION

Norton, Ohio, became a township in 1818; founded on some of the finest land, it was acknowledged as an excellent agricultural community dotted with various large farms. These farmlands produced corn, livestock, wheat, oats and cattle. But with that type of production came some tragedy. Many farmers with multiple children worried about their crops and how they were going to feed and sustain their families. Sometimes the burden became too much for some of the farmers and the only way they could see to end their burden was to take their own lives. Barns easily caught fire by careless acts, lightning or lanterns. People would steal from them, including chicken theft. One of the worst times for farm burglaries was in 1886. Barn raising was an especially exciting time of year but was also the most dangerous. As men fell timbers, many a tragedy would occur. The hoisting of entire heavy barn sides might collapse on the men, sometimes to the horror of observing family members. Most homes had a water well, which in itself was a liability for young children. But even some adults were known to drown in what seemed to be such a small space.

Norton also had coal mining in the southwest corner, and early industries included gristmills, sawmills, tanneries and blacksmith shops. Many of the early industries were ripe for accidents, including fires, falls and assorted injuries each unique to its enterprise.

Norton has many waterways coming through the township (now a city) and made for easy access for swimming at the turn of the century and today. But with water can come the inevitable mishaps and drownings. As industry

Map of Norton.

spread, along came rock quarrying and the subsequent deep-water lakes left behind. These were ripe for illegal nighttime swims and daytime trespasses by early youth.

The Atlantic and Great Western Railroad runs the entire length of the city from west to east, and before there were early warning signs, signals and gates, it was up to each individual to be on the lookout for the mighty monster, the locomotive. Many a horse and buggy, along with its occupants, never made it across the tracks, only to be dragged, run over or narrowly missed. Later, when the car was invented, numerous messy mishaps occurred while crossing those very same rails.

Norton boasted its own airport that had many names over the years, including Ling Field, Barberton Airport and even Sherman Airport. With accessible local flight came tragedy for numerous young fliers. And even the airport itself was not immune to its own frightful demise.

Over more than two hundred years, Norton has had its share of misdeeds and tragedy, some of which include murder, fraud, stabbings, neglect, shootings, hit skips and even a dynamiting incident.

Before you take the tour through some of the ugly and profound, let's understand the places in the township where these events took place. Inside you will find references to different areas in the Norton boundary. These are hamlets or crossroads that locals still refer to today. Each hamlet originally held its own specific industries, stores and schools. These hamlets include Norton Center, Loyal Oak, New Portage, Johnson's Corners, Hametown, Western Star and Sherman. For this reason, a map has been provided for the reader to more easily comprehend where each activity can be found. Many of the roadways that are mentioned are not on the map or might have been changed, but rest assured that all of the activities that have been listed are indeed fact.

So, let us begin our journey to some of Norton's most notorious, infamous, frightening, curious and sometimes sad incidents.

1

MURDERS

Momma Knows Best

Two miles south of Johnson's Corners in Summit County, Ohio, Norton Township, a gunshot sounded one cold January night. A bullet in her right temple and left for dead, Minnie Berndt, seventeen, of Hametown lay in a hay mow on the Leo Deibel farm.

For four months, Berndt lay dead, and when she was found, the local coroner, L.B. Humphrey, described the scene. He reported that her extremities had all been devoured by rats, including her scalp. All that was left was her hair, which was partly used to identify the body, along with an identifying mark on her shoulder from a previously infected wound. Inside the raincoat that she had been wearing was a mass of putrefaction. Inside that putrefied mass of what was once Minnie Berndt was discovered the bones of her six- to seven-month-old fetus. A local doctor, J.S. Davison, remarked that an inspection on the inside of her skull revealed nothing left inside.

Berndt was working at the Barberton Pottery Factory, where she met Deibel, who was in a temporary position. Their friendship deepened, and they eventually fell in love. Berndt told coworkers that she was going to quit her job and marry Deibel. Later, she took a position working for the Diamond Match Factory, having said nothing more about being married.

Left: Leo Deibel. Akron Beacon Journal, *Newspapers.com*.

Right: Minnie Berndt, murdered by Leo Deibel to cover their sin. Akron Beacon Journal, *Newspapers.com*.

Berndt was said to have love and devotion for the older man of twenty years. She gave her innocence to him. Knowing that Berndt was in a delicate condition, Deibel was willing to marry her, and they had planned to elope. Deibel's mother forbade him from marrying the much younger girl.

On January 28, 1906, Leo Deibel picked up Minnie Berndt and together they went to the local town of Barberton then later to the Deibel farm. Deibel made a bed for Berndt in the upper hay mow of the family barn and tended to her for three days, trying to devise a plan for their eventual departure or marriage. Berndt could no longer take it. They were to elope, or she would tell Deibel's mother the whole tale. Berndt said that she just wished that Deibel would kill her if they could not marry because she could never return home to her family.

On January 31, Deibel went through with his plan to take care of the problem. He loaded his Winchester .28-caliber rifle, climbed atop a beam in the barn about ten feet from the sleeping girl. Using the moonlight to guide him, he took aim and shot poor Minnie in the left temple. He never went to see if she was dead but went inside the farmhouse and went to bed. He had intended to either burn down the barn or to bury the body, both of which he ended up being too panic stricken to do.

Family members of Berndt began to become concerned for her whereabouts and started looking for her. They even questioned Deibel, who lied and said that he had dropped her off in Barberton, where she got a ride into Akron to get a job. As the months progressed, the stench in the barn became overwhelming The farm handyman, Henry McMahon, had complained to Deibel about the smell, but Deibel just shrugged it off as dead rats. It wasn't until Deibel's younger brother was hoisted into the upper hay mow by McMahon to look for chicken eggs that the discovery was made. Walter Deibel, age eight, discovered the reeking mass under a foot of hay and told McMahon what he had found.

McMahon hitched up his team and headed south to Clinton, where he met up with his friend Cameron Tope. He stayed the night with Tope, and in the morning, they headed to Barberton to make a report with Marshal Ferguson. With two officers in tow, they observed the scene at the farm. Deibel came right out and said that he was being framed and he was not guilty of anything. The marshal then became suspicious of him and continued to keep surveillance of the young man. Eventually, Deibel was arrested and taken to the Akron Jail.

Deibel's mother was the first visitor to the jail, where they cried together. Mrs. Deibel wept loudly and, according to the *Akron Beacon Journal*, said, "Oh, if I would only have allowed him to marry the girl. It is too late now. If I had not objected to him marrying the girl all would have been well today, and my boy would have been a free man."

After a lengthy and notorious trial, Deibel plead guilty to the murder and was sentenced to a life of hard labor at the Ohio Penitentiary.

Mother Deibel continued to visit her son on a weekly basis to consult him about how to run the farm.

In 1916, 133 prisoners were paroled or given a final release from the Ohio Penitentiary by the board of administration. Leo Deibel, who had been tried and convicted of second-degree murder, was one of them.

Two years before Leo killed his girlfriend, his father had died by suicide, and neighbors pointed out that Deibel's father had been in the same predicament. Deibel's father, too, wanted to wed the girl he had gotten pregnant, but his parents forbade it, and he took to drinking, and eventually, on February 19, 1946, at 12:54 p.m., at the age of fifty-nine years, two months and ten days, Leo Lewis Deibel shot himself in the head.

THE SITTER KNOWS BEST

"I feel sorry about it now. I'm guilty. I don't care what happens to me. I didn't want to find another job. I knew I couldn't hold it. I got pretty upset, so I decided to take the baby's life." These were the words spoken by Rochelle Posey, twenty, in June 1962 after murdering a child in her care.

Posey was set to lose her babysitting job and her place to live because she let her boyfriend constantly come over to visit and one night even let him stay without the consent of Ruth Magier, the baby's mother.

Ruth Magier, after seeing the young man's bicycle behind the house the evening before and still there in the morning, called Posey from her job and inquired about it. This was enough for Magier to fire the girl. Posey became upset and took Michael Magier, thirteen months, from his crib, put him on the sofa and proceeded to strangle him with a stocking. She admitted that it took twenty minutes for the baby to die. Fortunately, during this horrific event, none of the other Magier children were at home. They were vacationing with grandparents. When the parents of little Michael were notified of the deed, both went into a state of shock and were hospitalized; it was eventually confirmed that they were both in fair condition.

Earlier in the year, Magier had gone to an employment bureau in Barberton, where she hired Posey to care for her four children. She did not check Posey's references because she was told that the girl was a good worker.

The phone call to Posey was what set her off because she said that Magier had fired her, which meant that she could no longer see her boyfriend and she knew that she could not hold any other job, as she had lost many in the past. Posey was also fearful of her own parents' reaction. At one point, Magier had come home unannounced to find the house in disarray, the boyfriend on the sofa and little Michael crawling around on the floor in a soiled diaper.

Asked by the police why Posey turned herself in, she distractedly commented without emotion that it was the right thing to do and she was supposed to. She also said that she wanted to be locked up.

By this time, Posey was facing a first-degree murder charge. She was also evaluated at the Lima State Hospital by Dr. J.O. Crisp and declared sane to stand trial. Doctor Crisp stated that Posey was not insane but was a "moron" with the IQ of fifty-five.

Posey admitted on the courtroom stand that killing the baby was the only way she could see to be "put away" in a detention home. Defense attorneys O. Henri Corvington and Kenneth B. Baker related a story about how

Posey had a rough childhood and how she would purposefully get into trouble so that she could go back to the detention home where people were kind to her.

Mrs. Lutherine Posey, forty, Rochelle's mother, admitted in court that she never even wanted her daughter or her seven other brothers and sisters. Ralph Posey, Rochelle's father, said he would beat the girl because she couldn't learn to read or do her math. The other kids would call her dumb and she had to be protected from getting beat up by the kids at school.

Posey was sentenced to life at hard labor at the Women's Reformatory in Delaware, Ohio, and escaped being executed by the electric chair, for which she was thankful.

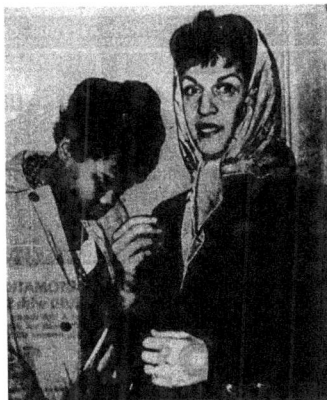

Rochelle Posey with Deputy Rita Kaster. *Akron Beacon Journal, Newspapers.com.*

Common pleas judges at the time had pleaded to have mercy granted on the girl because she had the mentality of a child between eight and twelve.

Posey died in Akron, Ohio, in 2008

DIRTY SECRETS

A farmhand on Medina Line Road in Western Star by the name of Rudy Tekancic came across a gruesome scene as he walked up to what appeared to be an abandoned automobile. Said to be going to Akron to an outdoor market for vegetables and fruit, instead Peter D. Baltic, sixty-one, and his stepdaughter Katherine Plavsity, twenty-three, were found dead inside the Packard Sedan.

In Baltic's hand was a .38-caliber revolver. Plavsity had a gunshot wound to the left side of her head. Baltic was slumped forward in the driver's seat with a gunshot wound to the left side of his head. Medina County coroner Theodore A. Cross ruled it a murder/suicide. Authorities determined that Baltic was not carrying a wallet and there was no money found in the car.

Baltic was the father of ten children and had been married three times. Oddly, all of the adult children were still living at the ninety-six-acre farm on Hametown Road in Sherman.

Katherine Plavsity, twenty-three, and her stepfather, Peter D. Baltic, sixty-one. Akron Beacon Journal, *Newspapers.com*.

Baltic farm as it stands today. *Author photograph*.

Deputy Fred Bailey (*left*) and Sheriff Robert L. Smith of Summit County inspecting the car where Plavsity and Baltic were discovered. Akron Beacon Journal, *Newspapers.com.*

Plavsity was the daughter of his current wife, Mildred, and Baltic had been overheard to say that he was angered by the young men that would come around to court her

Jerry Irby, eighty, who grew up in Norton, remembers his parents talking about the murder for years. His parents, James and Grace Irby, remembered Baltic to be quite the womanizer and a drinker. Rumors swirled that he had gotten Plavsity pregnant.

Baltic and Plavisity were both buried at the Lakewood Cemetery in Akron, leaving family members to wonder about the whole affair.

SELF-DEFENSE

Married at fourteen, raising six kids, trapped in an on-and-off relationship and pregnant with her seventh child, Alice Sammons, thirty-two, took things into her own hands in July 1963.

Returning from work at midnight from her shift at Babcock and Wilcox in Barberton, she heard a knock at her door. At the door appeared her husband wanting to make up after having left her a week prior. The husband, Oliver Sammons, twenty-eight, after arguing with his wife and falling asleep on the couch, was awakened and found the muzzle of a shotgun to his face. Alice Sammons was charged with second-degree murder.

All of this chaos took place in Barberton at the home of Mrs. Sammons's brother and sister-in-law, but the family tragedy continued as twenty people assembled at the home of Mrs. Michael Kindel Sr. of Woodlawn Drive in Norton. The people in the home included the younger Kindels and their children, the elder Kindels and Mrs. Sammons's seven sisters and brothers.

Mrs. Kindel Sr. was a sitter for Sammons's children while she was at work. The children would return to their home in Barberton in the morning with their mother after spending the night with Grandma.

Mrs. Sammons worked to take care of her children, using all of her money to feed and clothe them even though they never seemed to have enough.

In October 1963, after testifing before a grand jury exposing years of abuse and creating no doubt that the shooting was in self-defense, Alice Sammons's charges were dropped.

Defense of Insanity

Evelyn Bailey, a Norton resident and mother of five, was found shot to death in April 1970, her bullet-riddled body found alone in a car in Youngstown. Bailey had been shot in the back, arm and chest. When Bailey's five-year-old son, Kenneth, was asked what happened, he reported that his mom and Andrew Torres went to a wooded area to target practice. He said his mother fell after being shot. Torres later took the boy to one of Bailey's neighbors, but Bailey was not with them.

Calls came into the Youngstown Police Department about a sick person just sitting in a car. Deputy Coroner W.R. Johnson of Mahoning County said the woman had been dead for at least six hours due to a homicide.

Bailey's husband, William, who worked for Goodyear Aerospace, claimed that Torres was a family friend. Torres had been staying at the Fosters Motel on Cleveland-Massillon Road in Norton and was employed by the City of Barberton sewer department.

Police were not clear where the shooting actually took place, as the boy could not lead them directly to the spot. Kenneth did give some excellent clues to follow in the mystery. He said that the man used his mom to target practice by shooting at her shirt, and she fell down. Then Torres stood over his mom and fired three more times. He mentioned that there was a home nearby with a deer in the front yard.

The Summit County sheriff's office took over the case and arrested Andrew Torres, thirty-two. Torres claimed that the five-year-old boy was placing cans for target practice while Bailey was taking pot shots over Torres's head. The wooded area where the shooting took place was finally identified to be near Revere School in Richfield Township.

In June 1970, the Summit County grand jury returned an indictment of second-degree murder against Torres. Then the jury in the Torres-Bailey case in January 1971 found Torres not guilty by reason of insanity after a long trial and five hours of deliberation. The defense maintained that Torres's mind snapped from the strain of the incident. He was later bound over to the Lima State Hospital until he could be restored to sanity.

A follow-up article in the *Akron Beacon Journal* shed some light on the whole strange incident. A question was posed: If a person kills someone and is considered unstable then is finally deemed sane, should they go free?

HOT HEADS

Her death notice read like this, according to the *Norton Pride* in May 1975: "In a few short moments, Emma Pottle lost her life a victim of a gunshot wound on April 23. Who can fully understand the circumstances? Those few moments that can't be erased have shattered the lives of all who loved them both. Mrs. Pottle was born in Sample, Kentucky. She is survived by her husband, Charles; sons, Paul and David, students at Norton; brothers, William and Tommy Horsley of Dayton, O.; sisters, Mrs. Mary Ballash of Barberton, O and Mrs. Annabell Goffinet of Richmond Va."

Pottle was a victim at the hand of her husband, who was unemployed. They had been arguing in their car when Charles Pottle shot his wife, Emma Louise Pottle, fifty-nine, of Hillcrest Road with a .22-caliber pistol. Emma Pottle was found sprawled in the family driveway about 8:20 a.m., with trauma to her chest and head. Police surmised that she had crawled for help after being shot. She died forty minutes later in Barberton Citizen's Hospital.

Charles Pottle, sixty-one, offered no resistance when the officers came to arrest him, finding him sitting calmly on his bed. He was transported to the Summit County Jail and charged with aggravated murder. Lieutenant John Van Hyning of Norton said that Pottle was to be arraigned in Barberton Municipal Court and could potentially face life imprisonment or the death penalty if convicted. His bond was set at $50,000. In July 1975, Pottle was permitted to plead guilty to a lesser offense of voluntary manslaughter. He was also granted a presentence hearing by the Adult Probation Department. He died in Orville, Ohio, in March 1983 at the age of sixty-nine, after a long illness, eight years after the murder.

ROBERT BUELL

Born on September 10, 1940, accused murderer and rapist Robert Buell died by lethal injection on September 24, 2002. His last meal? One black unpitted olive.

In 1959, Buell graduated from Norwood High School in Cincinnati, Ohio. In 1961, he enlisted in the United States Navy and married a year later in Steubenville, Ohio. He had a daughter born in 1965 in Maryland and then was honorably discharged from the navy. He worked jobs such as an industrial salesman for Sherwin-Williams Paint Company and W.T. Grant Company in New York City and then moved to Norton and settled in Melody Village, a modest allotment of homes. There he worked as an assistant manager for Avco-Delta Mortgage Company in Akron and later as a loan officer and assistant cashier at the Akron Main Street branch of Centran Bank. By 1975, he was found working as a grant and loan specialist in the Akron Planning Departments rehabilitation program. In 1978, he was arrested in Uniontown, Ohio, for public indecency and disorderly conduct in connection with the incident and paid a fine.

In 1980, he and his wife divorced, and by the next year, he was identified by a thirteen-year-old Doylestown girl as the man who fondled her in her basement. That same year, a twelve-year-old girl disappeared from her home in Creston, Ohio. Tina Marie Harmon was found raped and strangled, and Buell became a suspect in the case. In 1982, a woman in Akron was abducted at knifepoint from a mall, sexually assaulted and robbed. She singled out Buell as her attacker. Krista Lee Harrison, eleven, was abducted from a park near her Marshallville home by a man driving a maroon van. Her body was found six days later in Holmes County strangled and raped. That same year, a twenty-six-year-old Barberton woman was abducted at gunpoint, beaten and assaulted. She, too, identified Buell as her attacker.

In 1983, a man in a maroon van came across two girls, ages twelve and thirteen, in Lodi and tried to abduct them at gunpoint. Buell was later identified as the possible abductor. In Jeromesville, Ohio, in Ashland County, Buell approached a girl in an alley while using his ex-wife's car, and witnesses saw the same car following school-age girls down a local street. Then a twenty-nine-year-old woman in East Liverpool, Ohio, was abducted at gunpoint and held as a prisoner at Buell's home, where she was sexually assaulted for three days. Buell was also a suspect in the case of Deborah Kaye Smith, ten, who disappeared from a Massillon carnival and was later found on the bank of the Tuscarawas River near Bolivar, Ohio. She, too, had been sexually assaulted and strangled. Continuing on with the year of 1983, a twenty-eight-year-old woman was abducted at gunpoint from Damascus, Ohio, at a gas station and taken to Buell's home, where she was handcuffed and sexually abused and tortured. She managed to escape, and Buell was then arrested and admitted to the attack. By 1984, Buell was sentenced to 121 to 320 years in prison as he plead no contest to sixteen felonies in the Damascus and East Liverpool abductions.

Was Buell guilty in all of the cases? Neighbors described him as knowledgeable and charming, always interested in projects. One neighbor described Buell as athletic and enjoying skiing and scuba diving. He was able to do anything. One of the younger neighbors described him as always talking and laughing. His home was described as immaculate. He went to neighborhood picnics and parties, went camping and was a family man by all appearances. He would go swimming, skiing, canoeing and hiking. He was said to spend a lot of time with the neighborhood children and was a delight to be around.

His professional career record was untarnished, and he was described as a positive person and a good employee. Peers in the companies where he worked described him as meticulous, confident, friendly but highly opinionated. But in retrospect he was also considered nasty, overbearing and arrogant. He was said to react to criticism by becoming hostile. He had a problem with female customers, especially those who were more forceful and knowledgeable. Neighbors reported seeing Buell coming home two and three times a day in his company car. Employers found out that he had been filling out his time sheets for appointments that he never made. It was later noted by Buell's former boss, Warren Walfish, that Buell took three and a

Right: Murderer and rapist Robert Buell. Akron Beacon Journal, *Newspapers.com*.

Below: The backyard of Robert Buell's Franklin Township home as authorities sift for evidence. Akron Beacon Journal, *Newspapers.com*.

Opposite: Map of Robert Buell's human hunt. Akron Beacon Journal, *Newspapers.com*.

half hours of vacation time on July 23, 1982, which was the same day that Krista Harrison's body was discovered in Holmes County.

It seems that Buell was not a happy man. He came from a broken home, one of verbal and physical abuse. Buell was tugged back and forth between his parents, Carter and Jacqueline Buell, creating a situation in which he was unable to pull himself away. During a custody dispute, Buell's father, Carter, claimed that Jacqueline did not want her two children and did not love them. The father

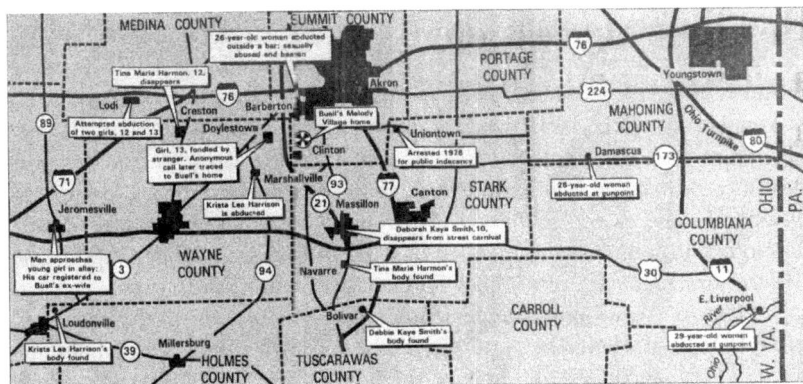

claimed that she had beaten the boy badly with a broom handle across his legs, breaking the handle, and also whipped him. Custody was denied to the father, and the mother then put the children into a boarding school, a place that Robert and his sister, Carole, said was dreadful. Later, as they were growing up, Carole stated that she could not understand what happened to her brother and wondered if he was holding their childhood traumas inside just waiting to explode. She described her brother as a normal guy, dating girls, going to drive-in movies and parties, bowling and dressing to the nines. She also stated that at one point her brother was abusing drugs and alcohol. She claimed that he would have blackouts. One of Buell's friends in school described him as fun loving and smart, receiving good grades easily, and was just a good friend. One of his romantic interests described him as generous, neat and handsome. She said that Buell was always good to her. It was after this that Buell decided to write off his family and start a new chapter. Although he did have one more thing to do and that was to show up in Seattle on a surprise visit to his father and his new wife, Opal's, home. Buell ran around freely in his father's sports car and jettisoned the beaches on his boat. Carter and Opal wanted Buell to stay in Seattle and go to the local university. He agreed then made off with a plane ticket, university registration money and money from his stepmother's purse.

Carter and Jacqueline Buell heard nothing from Robert for years, until two women contacted them requesting money for his legal fees. Buell by now had been arrested for the first of many crimes. Buell's ex-wife and his ex-girlfriend teamed up to help him by raising funds from a second mortgage on a home and signing a note for $12,000.

The undoing of Buell was when one of his tortured victims escaped. Reports by the *Akron Beacon Journal* described a panic-crazed young woman who burst from his Franklin Township home the morning of October 17, clothed only in an ill-fitting blue bathrobe, head shaved, handcuffs dangling from her left wrist. Franklin Township Police said that she had been abducted at gunpoint at about 10:15 p.m. the night before from a Mahoning County filling station and was handcuffed and forced to lie down in a van and then was driven to Buell's home in Melody Village. She had been ordered to undress, was handcuffed to a weightlifting bench and for the next eight to ten hours was forced to submit to and perform a series of sex acts with her captor. She was tortured with electrical shocks, had her head shaved and a plastic bag was taped over her head until she passed out. She was beaten on the chest and stomach with fists and a belt until she felt blood flowing internally. Finally, the woman was handcuffed and tied to a bed, facedown. About 8:00 a.m., Buell left for work, saying that he would be back in three hours. When he returned, the Franklin Township Police were waiting for him. The twenty-eight-year-old woman from Damascus, Ohio, had escaped and ran to a nearby neighbor's home, pleading for help. The neighbor woman opened her door and then shut it tight and bolted it, not knowing the circumstances.

FBI agents and three local police forces scoured Buell's 1978 maroon van looking for evidence. They searched the wooded area close to his home and dug around the shrubbery for any type of evidence that could be used to make a case. Agents turned to the home and took clothing that matched the description of the clothing of a twenty-nine-year-old woman who had been lured into a reddish-brown van and then abducted from Chester, West Virginia. The victim described her captor of three days at the home as a man six feet tall with grayish dark hair in his late forties. He had blue-green eyes and a skinny nose. Also taken as evidence was a light green bottle with a long neck that was used to sexually assault her. Discovered during the search were five white candles, a sixteen-ounce carton of white candle wax and a sixteen-ounce carton of white-orange paraffin. The Summit County coroner, William Cox, had confirmed that chunks of yellowish white wax containing bodily fluid was found near and under the body of Debbie Kaye Smith, one of the abducted and murdered girls. Evidence showed that the wax was used in the sexual abuse of the child.

Carpet fibers from the van were sent to the FBI laboratory in Washington, D.C., to see if they matched the ones found on Krista Lea Harrison. Carpet fibers found in the bedspread that Krista's body was wrapped in and the carpet fibers found on Tina Harmon's clothing were a match. In 2010, DNA evidence proved that Buell in fact did kill Tina Harmon. Semen on Harmon's clothing was analyzed with a ninety-six trillion chance that the DNA belonged to someone other than Buell.

Two other women who had been abducted in the past were said to have had their head and pubic hair shaved and were blindfolded, tortured with a waxy component and held captive for about a day and night. One was handcuffed and the other was in chains attached to rafters in a cellar-like room. Electrical cords were used to restrict one of the women. One woman was then dumped off the side of a road and the other was tied to a tree and succeeded in setting herself free. Buell was not ruled out as a suspect in these cases because of the similarities of others that he had committed and admitted to.

Now that Buell was in custody the authorities could narrow down some of the other cases that he was suspected of being involved in, including cases in Lodi and Columbus and in Terre Haute, Indiana.

More details surfaced about a man in a car that matched the description of the car that Buell's ex-wife owned. In Jeromesville, a young boy came into his home yelling about a guy in the alley trying to take a little girl. After the Harrison abduction and murder, citizens were on edge. A man in the home burst out to the alley and described the man as about thirty years old with dark hair and a mustache. He said that he was sure it was Buell. The girl that was approached was nine years old and was riding her bike in the alley. She said that a man got out of his car and was talking to her. He told her how pretty she was and asked where she lived. It was overcast that evening, and the man said that they could go inside a nearby building together and close an open window. Thankfully, the little girl said no and rode home to safety. The man who ran into the alley was able to get the license plate number of the car, and it came back to Robert Buell's ex-wife's car. After this incident was reported, other residents reported having seen a similar car slowly going down their streets.

Another eerie story came out of Doylestown in 1982, when a young girl would get repeated phone calls from a man talking nicely to her and asking questions about her school and even knew her name. Earlier that year, someone had broken into the family home and all that was missing was a photograph of the little girl. A tracer was put onto the phone line, and it could not identify where the phone calls were coming from. Then the calls abruptly stopped and started again. Then, again, the family home was burglarized and the only thing missing was the girl's purse. Her underwear drawer had been disturbed. Finally, a tracer tracked Buell's number to his home, but the name did not register at the time with the authorities. Because Buell's record of public indecency was expunged in 1978, the police had no record on which to further the investigation.

Police agencies had not closely monitored each other's reports and sources until one day a list was compiled after Buell had already been arrested. The pieces of the puzzle were finally coming together. Even the neighbors in Melody Village were concerned that Buell could be a suspect in all the cases. In 1980, after Buell's wife left him and moved out, the neighbors said that he had changed. He wore his hair longer and acted like he wanted to be a swinger. He even changed his mannerisms and his style of clothing. He even started spending time with the kids in the neighborhood. He would play loud music all day and night.

Three professionals evaluated Buell, including Phillip J. Resnick, MD, a forensic psychiatrist who had interviewed up to four hundred sex offenders for potential treatment; A. Nicholas Groth, a criminal psychologist; and Murray L. Cohen, PhD, a psychology professor at the Treatment Center for Sexually Dangerous Persons. All three admitted that it was possible for the same person to have committed the rape-murder of little girls and also the adult rapes. Clearly, they agreed that Buell was a sadist who enjoyed and became aroused by others' pain. As the aggression increased it sometimes culminated in death. Cohen referred to Buell as a "very, very disturbed person in the most ugly of manners in the human mind," according to the *Akron Beacon Journal*. All three professionals agreed that Buell's crimes showed elaborate preparation by choosing measures that were particular to the individual's vulnerability, readily having handcuffs available in his van and having his home prepared in advance for his next victim. A sadist such as Buell sees the victim as a symbol and not as a person, and the victims are somehow sexualized as an abandoning mother. Groth stated that when rapists let their captives go, it is often because they show a soft caring side to them so that the captor can see them as a real person. Being meticulously clean is part of the scenario, as many rapists have obsessive compulsive disorder and cleaning up plays a role in the rapes and abductions. Both abducted women said that they were told to shower and their clothing had been laundered. The house was then cleaned thoroughly as if in an effort to undo what had just been done.

In summary, Buell was the prime suspect in the murder and rape of Krista Lea Harrison in July1982, in Marshallville, Ohio. She had been looking for aluminum cans with a boy. She was dragged screaming into Buell's van. Her body was found six days later, having been strangled and raped with a vibrator. Fibers were found on Krista's body that matched fibers from the carpet in Buell's van. Paint matched the paint found on jeans that were left at the crime scene to paint in Buell's house. Buell had purchased customized van seats that were packaged in the same type of material used to discard the body by wrapping it around her legs. Also discovered was a wad of Krista's hair in a Budweiser towel, two pieces of cardboard box with bodily fluids and a shipping label sprayed over and a garbage bag with tape on it that had been taped on the dead girl's body. Neighbors reported that after the Harrison murder Buell had changed the appearance of his van and changed out the windows. In October 1982, Buell was charged with abduction and rape of a Columbia County woman, of which he pleaded no contest, as well as the abduction and rape of a woman from Chester, West Virginia. He was sentenced to 121 years in prison for those particular crimes.

Buell claimed that he was constitutionally violated at the trial, that he was given ineffectual counsel and was subjected to proprietorial wrongdoing and cruel and unusual punishment because the death penalty was on the table. Governor Bob Taft and the state and federal courts reviewed and upheld Buell's conviction and his sentence, saying that he had a just trial and satisfactory legal representation.

While Buell spent time in jail, protesters outside the Southern Ohio Correctional Facility said that research shows that the death penalty is unfair. They had posters and photos of other men executed, and candles were lit on the ground.

Buell's sister insisted that her brother was innocent and expected there to be a new trial because of new evidence that she claimed raised reasonable doubt. Buell's attorneys wanted to go before the Ohio District Court of Appeals in Cleveland, claiming that they had new evidence and wanted to stop the execution. Ohio governor Bob Taft refused the request, and the Ohio Parole Board was in agreement against leniency.

The morning of Buell's execution, he had bran flakes and milk and listened to the radio, and at 4:06 p.m., he ate his olive. His execution was seen by Krista Harrison's father, Gerald, and her two older brothers, Dana and Mark. They held tightly onto one another while keeping their eyes on the perpetrator. Buell refused eye contact. He spoke with guards and clenched his fist as he was being tied down to the gurney.

Buell's last spoken words were to the governor and the family of Krista Harrison. Reported by the *Akron Beacon Journal*, these were his final words:

> *I had invited the governor to be here today. He obviously didn't come. Governor, if you can't bring your wife to your workplace, you are obviously ashamed of what you do. If you are ashamed of what you do then you shouldn't be doing it. Jerry and Shirley* [Krista's mother]. *I didn't kill your daughter. The prosecutor knows that…and they left the real killer out there on the streets to kill again, and again and again. So that some good can come from this, I ask that you continue to pursue this to the end. Do not*

let the prosecutor to spin this out of focus and force them to find out who really killed your daughter. That's all I have to say.

Buell closed his eyes as his Adam's apple jutted in and out while the lethal drugs were being administered. The doctor in charge pronounced Robert Buell dead. Buell's death was pronounced by the warden at 10:30 a.m. He was buried in a $200 state-purchased coffin in a $50 suit, and his body was placed in an inmate cemetery in Chillicothe.

A No-Good Boyfriend

The autopsy report for twenty-two-year-old Sandra Burger, who weighed only ninety pounds and was a bit over five feet tall, reads like a horror story. The horror begins knowing that it was from a ferocious beating by her boyfriend, Mark Headley, on March 22, 1982.

Mark J. Headley, twenty-eight, was a former Norton High School graduate and the son of a former Barberton councilman, ex–state legislator, lawyer and former Barberton policeman David L. Headley. Sandra Burger was living with her boyfriend on Harvard Avenue in Barberton when she decided she was done with the relationship and wanted to move out, explaining to her mother, Connie, that she was fearful of Headley and wanted to move back home. Burger enlisted the help of her sister Theresa Burger. Sandra Burger was afraid of what Headley might do if there was a confrontation, so she made arrangements to move out while Headley was at work at his job as a Metro bus driver. After Burger moved out, Headley showed up at Theresa Burger's house, where the sisters were having dinner. Headley asked to talk with Sandra, and they left the house together. Sandra never returned. Connie called Headley's house at around 11:00 p.m., and he told her that Sandra was sleeping.

The following morning, a call came into the Barberton Fire Department's rescue unit for assistance from a friend of Headley's, explaining that there was a girl in the Headley home who would not wake up. When the unit arrived, it was apparent that Burger was already dead. No knife or bullet wounds were found on the body by the coroner's investigator. Headley remained at the home while police arrived, and he surrendered to them.

By March 27, Headley was charged with the murder and beating death of Burger and was released from the Summit County Jail after posting a $50,000 property bond using his father's property as collateral. On March

31, Headley was indicted by a Summit County grand jury for aggravated murder. On April 2, Headley pleaded innocent of the charges. By June 17, Headley had been sentenced to fifteen years to life after having pleaded guilty in the beating death of Burger. Headley was able to plead guilty to the lesser charge after plea-bargaining with the Summit County prosecutor's office.

After serving twenty-five and a half years in prison, Headley came up for parole. Five people, including two sisters of Burger and a retired Barberton police lieutenant who was at the scene of the crime, asked the board to keep Headley in prison. Also asking for Headley to be kept in prison were 438 signatures on petitions and 32 letters to the parole board. Theresa Burger White wanted the parole board to understand how much her sister meant to their family and how all she wanted her sister to do was get out of a bad relationship. She talked about the ruin that this murder had caused to her family. She also made it clear that Headley did not have a clean record in prison after causing all kinds of havoc. Headley was known to have a discipline problem and at one point was moved to a more secure prison. He was also disciplined for gang activities, drug use and threatening other inmates. The defense attorney, Barry Wilford, claimed that Headley, a bodybuilder, was on steroids at the time of the murder and had psychotic behavior that led to his unusual behavior. He said that in the past two years Headley had been attending Bible classes and had no disciplinary actions against him.

The retired police officer, Ernie Penko, who was the first to see Sandra's body said that Sandra was "beat to a pulp." He said a person falling to their death from the seventh floor of a building still would not have been in as bad condition. He felt that Headley should have been given the death penalty. Connie Burger Leidel said that if Headley were to get out on parole and get involved with another woman that she better not think of leaving him because he would resort to violence. Headley got his parole. He was given five years of probation and drug screens and was to follow all laws.

Mark Headley shown here in 1971. All-Metro Squad on defense, football. *NHS Yearbook.*

Headley was a high school football player in the '70s and played as a defensive lineman. His coach described him as the hardest hitter on the team. Headley weighed in at 188 pounds in 1971. By the time of Burger's murder, Headley was a whopping 260 pounds of pure muscle with a six-foot frame. Burger's body had seventy contusions and abrasions on every inch of her five-foot frame. Her entire scalp was one large hematoma with subarachnoid hemorrhages on both cerebral hemispheres. She suffered two liver lacerations and contusions on the duodenum and pancreas, as well as a contusion to her right lung, which was found to have partial fragments of skeletal tissue. She also suffered from acute congestion of the heart, all due to the beating that Headley had bestowed on her.

In 2012, three months before his probation was to expire, Headley was charged with a DUI after crashing into a sheriff's cruiser and injuring the officer in Florida. Headley had moved to Florida to be near his daughter, Brenda Davidson. According to the Florida Department of Corrections, Headley was sentenced for that crime in 2015 and is still in custody.

THE VISITOR FROM HELL

Assuming the two might get married in the future, Homer Straub, fifty, of Sterling, Ohio, spoke about his daughter, Judith Straub, eighteen, and her boyfriend, William Lavaco, twenty-one, of Doylestown. It was the last time he'd see either of them alive.

Straub and Lavaco had been seen last at 2:00 a.m. on Saturday, August 8, 1977, talking to an unknown man at the Sun Valley Inn in Doylestown. The unidentified man was found, questioned by Norton Police chief Forrest Diefendorff and then released. By Monday, missing persons reports were filed on both individuals by their families.

Lavaco's car, a light blue 1975 Monte Carlo was later found in the Silver Creek Metropolitan Park. Inside, the authorities found Straub's shoes and her purse with $400 inside. Straub had given Lavaco $700 to purchase a truck, and it was determined that Straub was probably the driver of the Monte Carlo, since Lavaco had given her the car. The truck was located at the Sun Valley Inn.

Divers from the Doylestown Fire Department and the Norton Police Department searched a pond and through underbrush in the park with metal detectors. In 1977, when the disappearances took place, the park was made up of 486 acres of mostly undeveloped land. A search on foot did not locate the pair, so an aerial search was ordered, and after about an hour, the pilot confirmed the sighting of two bodies under a tree near the parking lot.

Left: William Lavaco; *Right*: Judith Straub. *Public domain.*

Once the bodies were located after walking through five-foot-high weeds, it was discovered that the couple were both shot in the neck pointblank with a shotgun, execution style. Both individuals were clothed. Lavaco was on his back, and Straub was facedown and barefoot. There were no spent shells at the scene, no weapon and no motive.

Leads came into the Norton Police Department, and fifteen people were questioned within days of the murder. One promising lead was that an argument had occurred at the Sun Valley Inn on the Saturday night that the couple were seen there. The argument took place between the unknown male and the couple. Robbery was ruled out as a motive because of all the cash that was found in Straub's purse.

The murders happened on August 8, and by August 17, the Norton Police Department had given three polygraph tests and spoken to several individuals, some repeatedly, all while awaiting results from the state crime laboratory on the vehicles. By August 30, Chief Diefendorff said that he had two detectives working on the case full time, including overtime and lots of legwork. By this time seven more lie detector tests had been given.

By September 1977, two banks in Wayne County, Ohio, were taking donations for a reward in the killings in the hopes of raising at least $5,000. By October, $1,000 had been donated, and by January 1978, the full $5,000 had been raised, with the money going to the person who could provide information leading to the arrest and a conviction of the killer.

Previously, officers had cited Dennis Ray "Duff" Busson for having an open container of beer outside of a service station. Lavaco had handed

Akron Beacon Journal file phot

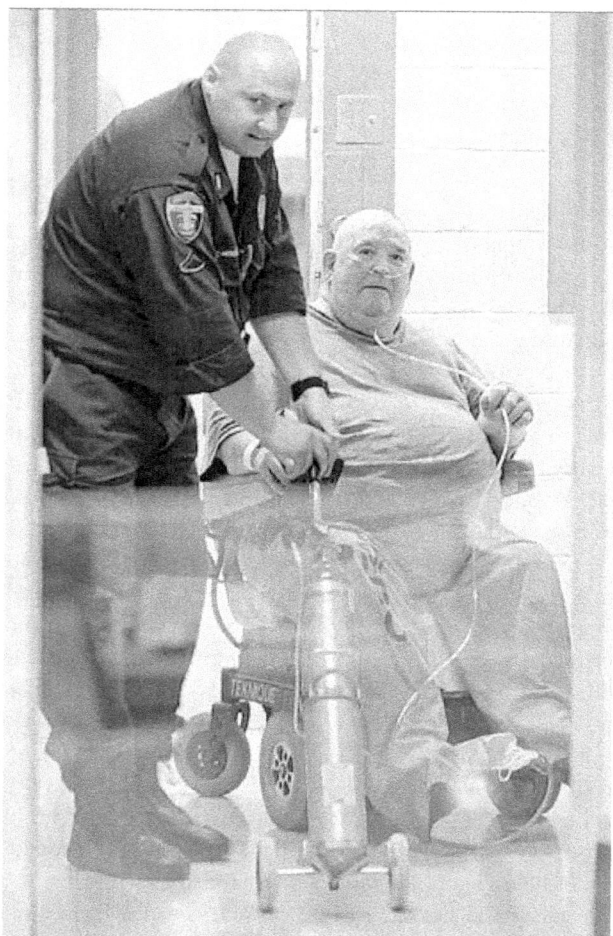

Edward Wayne
Edwards (*right*),
seventy-six, in
1962. Akron
Beacon Journal,
Newspapers.com.

Busson the can, and Busson blamed Lavaco for the arrest. Busson was released the same day with a five-dollar bond. By this time, some evidence in the murders was coming in. The twenty-gauge shot gun that was used had been loaded with bird shot and a slug, which was normally used to hunt deer.

Meanwhile, Busson was the prime suspect in the case as detectives were finding more and more evidence but no witnesses who would come forward. Warrants were issued for Busson's arrest, and he appeared before Barberton Municipal Judge Adam Gadanac Jr. Bond was set for Busson at $50,000 on each charge. During Busson's arrest, he called his mom and said, "Don't worry mom, I didn't do it. I'll sue them this time." This was quoted in the *Akron Beacon Journal*.

Busson was described as an All–Wayne County League football player who was unafraid of anyone because of his strength and size. Busson's football coach said that he was one of the most elite players he ever coached. Busson played fullback at Chippewa High School from 1967 through 1971.

Both the Lavaco and Straub families were relieved to know that the police had someone in custody. In June 1979, Busson was to appear before Barberton Municipal judge John Judge. During his appearance, a seventeen-year-old boy testified that he witnessed Busson kill the couple in cold blood. Jay Starcher said that he was inside the park barn when he saw it happen. He claimed that he and a friend were on the second floor of the barn busting beer bottles when he heard a car come into the park. He claimed that two men and a woman were in the car and further stated that a truck came pulling into the lot and had blocked the front of the car. He also said that Busson was driving the truck and walked up to the car and started an altercation. He said that Busson said if the people messed with him, he would kill them, and there was considerable yelling going on regarding $500 and the keys to a vehicle. Starcher mentioned, too, that the name Duff was overheard. Starcher said that Busson was carrying something long, but he could not tell what it was. Then he said that Busson opened the car door, and the car's driver jolted back and there was a loud noise like a shot. After that, a woman and a man fled there on foot. When the woman turned and faced Busson, Starcher said that he heard another shot and the woman collapsed to the ground. When asked if Starcher was sure it was Busson, he replied that he had no doubt in his mind. Being cross-examined by the defense attorney, George Pappas, Starcher confessed to being a heavy drug user and had used weed that day. Starcher didn't say anything about what he had witnessed until he had been picked up by Norton Police for burglary, of which he was not charged. When asked on the stand why he was arrested by the police, Starcher responded that he couldn't remember, leading the defense attorney to question why he could remember people being killed two years ago but not why he was recently detained by police. Starcher claimed that he was an upright citizen. The attorney then wanted to know if he just wanted something for his testimony, implying the award money that was up for grabs. Also on the stand were two criminals who were serving time in jail who testified against Busson, Randy Thompson and Mark Smeddon.

In August, the Summit County grand jury began hearing testimony on the charges against Busson. Starcher was also to testify. The grand jury refused to indict Busson, giving no reason why they came to this decision. A "no bill" was returned, which meant that there was insufficient evidence to warrant a conviction. Busson was relieved as he was told the news and declared from the beginning that he never committed the crimes and had no idea who did. George Pappas, Busson's attorney, was not in the least bit surprised at the grand jury's findings. He felt all along that there just was not enough evidence of any wrongdoing.

Jurors had insisted on seeing the place where the murders took place. They determined that there was no way that Starcher could have possibly seen what he claimed happened that moonlit night from the barn where he was standing.

In April 1980, Busson made good on his threat to sue. He had a $1 million suit for punitive damages. Attorney Bruce Wilson took the case on behalf of Busson and wanted to bring action against every person involved. The officers on the case had damaged Bussons reputation and self-esteem and cost him money in his own defense. Wilson sought $11,000 from the officers for attorney fees that were used to defend Busson. The suit named officers Franklin Tomblin and Robert Boord. Also named in the suit were Jay Starcher, Mark Smeddon and Randy Thompson. Busson stated that he never saw a dime from any of it and that the jailbirds didn't have a dime to their names. The suit against the officers was dismissed on a legality, since Busson was still the prime suspect. After thirty-some years, the Norton Police Department apologized to Busson, and Busson stated in 2020 that he is still harassed now and then, along with his kids in school

It wasn't until about thirty-three years later that serial killer, arsonist, robber and rapist Edward Wayne Edwards, seventy-six, fessed up to the killing. Edwards only confessed to the murders of Straub and Lavaco because he wanted to serve his upcoming prison sentence in Ohio and not in Wisconsin, where he was charged for another double murder. He was sentenced to death by lethal injection on March 8, 2011, and was said to be unbothered by the sentence. His execution was scheduled for August 31, 2011, but before the state had a chance to execute him, he died at the age of seventy-seven of natural causes while in the Ohio Department of Rehabilitation and Corrections Medical Center in Columbus, Ohio. Edwards suffered from diabetes, heart problems and leukemia.

ROBBERY, RAPE AND MURDER

In 1986, a gruesome crime that started in Akron concluded with the horrendous deaths of two University of Akron girls whose bodies were discovered in Norton just a fourth of a mile from Akron-Wadsworth Road.

Dawn McCreery, twenty, who grew up in North Ridgeville, liked to party and especially enjoyed punk rock and rock music. She loved to draw and write poetry and was the rush chairperson for her sorority, Alpha Delta Pi, at the University of Akron. She was studying fashion and marketing. McCreery had just gotten a new apartment nearby and was in her sophomore year of college. Wendy Offredo, twenty-one, from Bath, was a junior at the University of Akron and loved to socialize and was a fun-loving person. She was majoring in textiles and wanted to travel and work as a buyer in her field. Her former boyfriend Greg Cable dated Offredo while attending Firestone High School and couldn't understand why anyone would want to hurt her. He said that Offredo was involved with synchronized swimming, National Honor Society and gymnastics. She worked at the service desk at the Summit Mall Woolworth's Department Store and was a part-time model, as well as a part-time worker for a local tanning company. Both girls worked for the Brown Derby in Montrose as waitresses. There they were described as hard workers, responsible and well liked.

On the night of September 1, 1986, the girls made plans to go to a night out at Portage Lakes after work to party at the Harbor Inn. They got off work between 11:00 p.m. and midnight, changed clothes and drove together in Offredos black Fiero. Driving on the expressway in Akron heading south, a piece of concrete was dropped from an overpass where it crushed the windshield of the car. The concrete was dropped from the Stoner Street I-77 overpass. Offredo had been injured by glass, and they pulled over to the side of the road. They were offered a ride to a pay phone so that Offredo could call her mother and the police department. She called the Fairlawn Police Department, thinking they were in that jurisdiction. Fairlawn passed the call

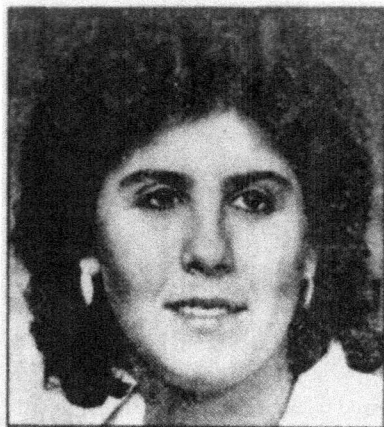

Dawn McCreery and Wendy Offredo. Akron Beacon Journal, *Newspapers.com.*

along to Copley who in turn passed it on the Akron Police Department. The phone calls were made at 12:15 a.m., and Offredo's mother and the Akron Police found the disabled car around 1:20 a.m., but the girls were not there.

With intentions of dropping the concrete block onto a car and robbing the occupants, Richard Cooey, nineteen; Clint Dickens (who dropped the block), seventeen; and Kenny Horonetz, eighteen, had their victims. When their fiendish plot was complete, the trio of boys had driven onto the freeway and pulled up behind the girls' car, where they accepted a ride to a pay phone in an empty parking lot in Hawkins Plaza at Hawkins Avenue and Wooster Road. Offredo's mother, Geri Muck, asked to talk to one of the men who was supposedly rescuing the girls and said that she did not have a good feeling about the situation. She described the man's voice as lacking any personality, and this made her uneasy. Wendy did not sound frightened at the time, and she overheard McCreery talking to the young men in the background.

Muck, after finding the abandoned car, filed a missing persons report and was up all night waiting for her daughter to return home. Wendy did not show up, nor did she call the next day at her job, so Muck immediately knew that something was terribly wrong. The young man on the phone had promised to bring the girls back to the car, but instead, Cooey had pulled a knife on them while Horonetz was ordered to tie up McCreery's hands. Horonetz, wanting nothing more to do with this loathsome situation, demanded to be let out of the car. Then the girls were driven down a dirt road just west of the Rolling Acres Mall and ordered to exit the car.

Above: Wendy Offredo's Pontiac Fiero was damaged when a concrete block was thrown from Akron's Stone Street Bridge. Akron Beacon Journal, *Newspapers.com*.

Right: Richard Cooey in 1986 being arraigned for the murder of two college girls. Akron Beacon Journal, *Newspapers.com*.

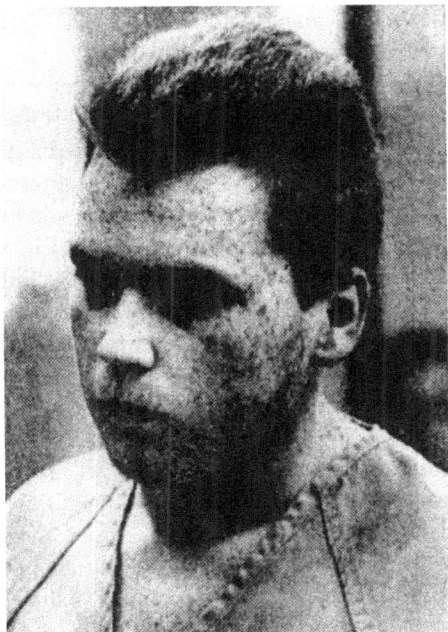

Cooey raped McCreery while Dickens raped Offredo. Then Cooey raped Offredo while Dickens raped McCreery. At this point, Cooey had called out Dickens's name, which made him angry. Dickens took hold of a billy club that had been lying on the car hood and began angrily striking a tree with it. After being raped, the girls were ordered back into the car while Cooey and Dickens decided to murder them. Dickens suggested that they kill the girls because they knew his name. Cooey then grabbed Offredo in a choke hold and strangled her until she was unconscious. Then he proceeded to tie her feet together with a red bandanna. Dickens then clubbed McCreery with the billy club when she made an attempt to get away. Cooey tied a shoestring around Offredo's neck, and Dickens tied another around McCreery's neck. Both girls were then brutally beaten in the head with the billy club. The entire horrifying ordeal lasted more than three hours.

All of the jewelry was taken from the girls' bodies and put inside their purses. Cooey and Dickens then dragged the bodies off the roadway and into some weeds. They brushed the car tracks off the road with tree branches and departed to a nearby car wash to clean the blood off the car and themselves. They got rid of the purses but went back to retrieve them after finding out that the bodies had been discovered by a young man who was walking through the woods. The boys, along with Terry Grant, took the purses to Cooey's house, where they burned them. Terry Grant, nineteen, said that he was there when the purse burning took place, and this was when Cooey and Dickens fessed up to the awful deeds. Horonetz was in attendance for the burning and was eventually charged with obstruction of justice for helping to destroy the purses and for felonious assault. Grant also said that it was probably Cooey's idea to murder the girls and Dickens was just frightened. Grant admitted that he was astonished and speechless to hear what the two young men had done, saying that Cooey could be mean and had been in trouble with the law in the past. Grant was eventually charged with obstructing justice after not reporting to police what he knew about the case.

After a few days had passed, someone called to report that Cooey was trying to sell jewelry that belonged to the victims and named the street where Cooey lived. The police set up surveillance around Cooey's house while warrants were being obtained. One warrant was to search the house and the other was to arrest Cooey. Cooey tried to leave the house and was immediately arrested. Items belonging to the girls were taken from him and from his grandmother's car. More items were taken from the grandmother's house.

By this time, autopsies were completed on both girls and read like the horror story that it was. McCreedy had prominent brain swelling with subfalceal, uncal and cerebellar tonsillar herniation with collapse of the ventricles, multiple lacerations of the scalp, hemorrhage in the left mastoid air sinus and linear abrasions around the neck consistent with strangulation. Further, she suffered multiple contusions and lacerations of the face and neck, both hands and right forearm and left hip. Bilateral pulmonary edema and congestion occurred to her right lung. The final cause of death was listed as cardiorespiratory arrest due to brain swelling with herniation and collapse of ventricles due to blunt force trauma to the head. Offredo suffered brain swelling with uncal and cerebellar tonsillar herniation and collapse of ventricles. She also had diffuse subarachnoid hemorrhage and diffuse subdural hemorrhage with multiple acute contusions involving the inferior lateral aspect of the right frontal lobe, the orbital gyri of the left frontal lobe, the left and right temporal poles, the inferior lateral aspect of the left temporal lobe and the inferior aspect of the left occipital lobe. Further recordings show that she suffered from a fracture of the calvarium and base of the skull, frontal scalp hemorrhage, subpleural hemorrhages, visceral pleura, anterior, lateral and five lobes. Lacerations were found on the right front scalp right eyebrow with multiple contusions and abrasions. Possibly done postmortem, she suffered a stab wound to the neck and an X was carved on her stomach. She had hemorrhages to the thymus and petechial hemorrhages in the epicardium. The final report shows the cause of death as cardiorespiratory arrest due to brain swelling complicated by subdural and subarachnoid hemorrhage due to fracture of the calvarium and base of skull due to blunt force trauma.

Dickens was tried as an adult and found guilty and sentenced to life in prison. Since Dickens was a minor at the time, he could not be given the death penalty. Cooey waived his right to a trial by jury, and a group of judges was appointed to try him. Cooey was found guilty by the judges and sentenced to death for charges of aggravated murder, kidnapping, rape, aggravated robbery and felonious assault.

In 2003, Cooey was interviewed, and according to the *Akron Beacon Journal* and the *Columbus Dispatch*, Cooey, then thirty-six, stated, "Right now, all I can do is put forth legal arguments and say why they should not kill me legally, because morally I don't have a foot left, or a toe to stand on." At the time, he was serving his sentence in the Mansfield Correctional Institution before he was transferred to the Southern Ohio Correctional Facility in Lucasville, where he would eventually be executed. "If I was the victims' families, I'd want me dead," said Cooey. He also admitted to kidnapping, robbing and raping the sorority sisters: "I take full responsibility. I am guilty of every one of the 13 charges but the murders. That's legally. Morally, I am guilty of the murders, and I expressed that." Asked how he dealt with knowing of his imminent death, Cooey stated, "I've been mentally preparing for it for 12 years. You don't let it eat you up, but it's hard. I deal with it."

Cooey was able to get a stay within twelve hours of his execution because he was without legal representation in the weeks leading up to his execution date, and a federal appeals court removed two of his attorneys for allegedly overbilling and filing frivolous claims. In 2008, at the age of forty-one, Cooey was once again up for his death sentence, this time claiming that he was too fat to get the lethal injection humanely. Cooey was five foot seven and weighed in at 267 pounds. He was still waiting for a ruling on his appeal of the Ohio Supreme Court's dismissal of his complaint that the state's protocol for lethal injection could cause an agonizing and painful death. He wanted another stay of execution. His lawyers also argued that a migraine medication prescribed by a prison physician could reduce the effect of the anesthetic used as part of the three-drug lethal injection. The Ohio Board of Parole and Governor Ted Strickland refused Cooey's plea for clemency. He had a last meal of a T-bone steak with A-1 sauce, onion rings, french fries, four eggs over easy, toast with butter, hash browns, a pint of rocky road ice cream, a Mountain Dew and a bear claw pastry.

The McCreery family chose to witness the execution. The Offredo family and the Cooey family chose not to attend. When asked if he had any final words, according to Wikipedia, Cooey angrily said, "You [expletive] haven't paid any attention to anything I've said in the last 22½ years, why would anyone pay any attention to anything I've had to say now?" At 10:20 a.m., the warden signaled the start of the flow of drugs. One put Cooey to sleep, a second paralyzed him and a third stopped his heart. He tapped his fingers on the gurney as the process unfolded. He died at 10:28 a.m. on October 14, 2008. A black hearse parked in the courtyard then took his body to a mortuary. He was immediately cremated at the state's expense. According to his wishes, Cooey's ashes were taken to Ireland by his attorneys.

A REGULAR WHO DONE IT

A pool of blood on the cellar floor, a razorblade and blood on a neighboring rooming house door were the only signs of something gone wrong. What

Sheriff Bob Smith and a host of relatives had was the only evidence to a possible crime against Paul Centa, who was missing from his home. Family members were stumped. Centa's twenty-one-year-old daughter, Angelina, had last seen her dad on the couch in the living room the previous evening. His wife, Jennie, had already gone to bed.

Members of the Civilian Conservation Corp were on the lookout for sixty-two-year-old Paul Centa of Sherman. They searched wooded areas and ravines in a five-mile radius. Columbia Chemical plant coworkers of Centa's said that he carried large sums of cash on him, and it wasn't any wonder something like this could happen.

Later, a bloody hatchet was found in an icebox in the basement of the Centa home, and a large slash was found in a table. Bloody handprints were found on inside and outside doorknobs, a window shade and a table. Questions arose about whether this was suicide or foul play. New discoveries came about as Summit County sheriff Walter P. O'Neil took over the scene. Another daughter of Centas, Louise Durbin, of Doylestown, was quoted in the *Akron Beacon Journal* as having said, "I fear that he met with foul play. I know that some of his companions weren't so good."

By March 11, 1929, prosecutor Alva J. Russell said the case had hit a stone wall, and no likely attacker had been uncovered in the investigation. Centa's son, Paul Jr., posted a reward of $100 for any information regarding his father's disappearance. After eight weeks, Paul Centa's body was found by James L. Irby, forty-two, a farmer who lived nearby. The body lay near a fence row on the Edward Cox farm near where Centa lived. Centa's daughter Angeline, who identified the decomposed body, collapsed as neighbors carried her away from the area.

Dr. R.E. Amos, coroner, said that there was a three-inch slash to Centa's jugular vein and determined that the body had lain on its back for a long period of time and had been moved to where it was found. He said that the body had been stored in a dry, cool place because of the lack of mold on the clothing.

Centa was said to have concealed about $2,000 in a vegetable bin a few feet from his house. This led investigators to conclude that he was robbed and murdered when the money came up missing.

An argument took place between coroner Amos and Sheriff O'Neil. The sheriff was accused of washing his hands of the whole affair and wanting Centa's case to end with a suicide. The facts for murder were substantiated with physical and medical evidence, but the case was dropped with no further investigation.

(*Top to bottom*) Home of Paul Centa, searchers fan out looking for the body of Centa, inside the blood-spattered basement of Paul Centa. Akron Beacon Journal, *Newspapers.com*.

James Irby points out the body of Paul Centa to authorities after he was found along a fence row. Akron Beacon Journal, *Newspapers.com*.

Jerry Irby, the son of James Irby, told the author that he remembers his dad collecting the $100 reward for finding the body, which he said was a lot of money back then. He also reiterated that the case was closed and nothing else was ever investigated.

Them's Fightin' Words

Charges of voluntary manslaughter followed a preliminary hearing in Barberton Municipal Court for Joseph Zelei, nineteen, in November 1979. Zelei, who lived on Rock Cut Road, was charged with the October 19, 1978 fatal shooting of Ricky Westfall of Barberton.

During testimony, the sister of Westfall, Karen Westfall, said that her brother told her they were going to a party somewhere in Norton. A group of about fifteen took off in their cars from the Westfall home and headed to the Zelei home. When she arrived at the Zelei home, she claimed that there was a wild disturbance going on and she witnessed Thomas E. Salisbury of Barberton fighting someone. There had been some bad blood between Zelei and Salisbury before the fight broke out, with both men fighting over an alleged car accident and a mutual girlfriend, Renee Radovic.

Testimony continued, with evidence pointing to the fight being started by Salisbury, who had jumped out of his vehicle asking where Zelei was. At that point, Salisbury and others of his group began beating on Zelei. Fighting continued between Zelei's friends and Salisbury's friends. The fighting broke up when Zelei's older brother brought out a gun. The older brother demanded that Salisbury and his friends leave and said the police had been called and were on their way. Joe Zelei then got away from the crowd, ran into the house and got a shotgun and loaded it. He shouted for Salisbury and his buddies to get out. Salisbury and his friends challenged him, claiming that he wouldn't shoot. Salisbury brazenly grabbed the shotgun barrel and then let go as Zelei was backing away. That is when Westfall grabbed the gun and it went off, shooting Westfall in the groin. Westfall fell along with the gun. By this time, the Norton police had showed up along with the Norton Emergency Medical Service. The medical services tried to stabilize Westfall, who was hanging on by a thread. He was transported to Barberton Hospital, where he underwent surgery and died the next day. Zelei fessed up and was also taken to the hospital for injuries.

A charge of voluntary manslaughter was made, and bond was set at $25,000, of which Zelei posted 10 percent and was released. In 1980, the Barberton Municipal Court jury found Zelei innocent. The original charge was voluntary manslaughter. Zelei was charged with negligent homicide.

ALL OVER A GIRL

Near a private lake in Norton called Lake Dorothy unfolded a horrible tragedy of murder and suicide in August 1992. For four hours, Norton police barricaded the lane that ran back to the one-hundred-acre private lake owned by PPG (Pittsburgh Plate Glass Company).

Rodney James Motich, twenty-six, who lived on the lake lane Dorothy Avenue, was a graduate of Wadsworth High School, a neighboring community of Norton. He was going through a divorce and had moved in with his parents after leaving Florida. Motich was described by his brother as someone who liked to race stock cars and an army veteran, and he was described by friends as thoughtful and jovial. Motich was gunned down by his friend Robert K. Childress II, twenty-one, of Barberton. The tragedy was witnessed by Motich three-year-old daughter while loading his car for a relaxing trip to Sea World.

Motich and Childress were known as the "Crazy Eights," along with Motich's brother Greg. They raced at the Barberton Speedway on Clarks-Mill Road in Norton with a Malibu stock car, No. 8. They were all good friends. They were all slated to drive in a race that same week, when all of a sudden, Childress had a change of heart. Apparently, Childress was angry over a former girlfriend who had begun dating Motich. There didn't seem to be any bad blood up to that point. The ex-girlfriend of Childress just wanted nothing more to do with him after having dated less than a year.

On the day of the Sea World trip, Childress called Motich and claimed that he was not going to make it on his outing. Motich just dusted it off as some kind of joke. Then family members at Lake Dorothy noticed a strange car inside the gate of the park hidden behind a very large tree. Childress shot Motich with a high-powered World War II vintage 7.62 rifle from one hundred feet. When Motich's grandfather walked up to his grandson, he noticed that he was not moving and had blood spattered on him. The grandfather, Ivan Motich, heard a second shot. It was the fatal bullet for Robert K. Kenny Childress to his own head.

2

CHOO CHOOS, PLANES, AUTOMOBILES AND MANGLED MASSES

CHOO CHOOS

Crossing railroad tracks in a horse and buggy during the late 1800s seemed to be a risky proposition. The following are anecdotes of the dangers:

In 1894, Edith Hartzell of Norton Center was on her way home from Johnson's Corners when her horse stepped onto the rails when an eastbound train ripped the beast from the shaft of the wagon, leaving the buggy on the road. Hartzell survived, but the horse died instantly.

Because there was no whistle or any type of signal, John Wiser of Loyal Oak sued the Erie Company for $200 when his horse was hit by a train.

In 1889, John Forer of Sterling, Ohio, was bringing his nine-year-old granddaughter, Carrie Orr of Norton Center, home when along came an eastbound Nypano train, which plowed into the horse and buggy, killing all inside and tearing the buggy into shreds. According to the *Summit Beacon*, "The sad occurrence has cast a deep gloom over the neighborhood."

In 1909, an Erie passenger train in Norton Center struck the horse and buggy of Mrs. Troutman, William Reid and Mrs. Troutman's five-year-old daughter, Evaline. According to the *Cincinnati Enquirer*, "When the train reached Kent, blood and remnants of a woman's clothing were found on the tender." With her golden hair torn from her scalp, her head crushed, five-year-old Evaline was the first one of the three found by searchers. Reid had a crushed skull, and Mrs. Troutman was the only survivor.

Sound asleep and awakened by the derailment of sixteen train cars, in 1974, at 4:00 a.m. Mrs. J. Irby of Dorothy Avenue heard the ruckus loud and clear. Most people in the area were used to the trains coming and going and didn't hear this particular crash. The derailment happened under the Route 21 overpass near Eametown. Industrial accident workers showed great skill as they stepped into the wreck. The Norton Volunteer Fire Department also lent a hand and battled danger as alcohol that the train was carrying began to burn. Copley firemen also came to the scene, along with Barberton firefighters, who filled a 6,500-gallon tank truck four times to extinguish the blaze, as there was no water source in the area. Mrs. Irby also recalled another incident when one hundred cars full of livestock were derailed and animals were running rampant. Butchers were called in from all over to salvage what they could.

In 1890, M.A. Phalen of Kent, Ohio, was a brakeman for the NYP&O Freight. He was braking near New Portage when, unbeknownst to him, the entire section of cars broke loose. He scurried to the front of the rolling beast trying to turn the brakes on, dropped off the front and proceeded to have his left arm cut off up to the shoulder.

Another victim to add to the growing list of train accidents was Joseph Knecht. According to the *Akron Beacon Journal*, "For 20 rods along the track was scattered the mutilated flesh of Joseph Knecht of Loyal Oak. All of his clothes had been ripped from his body and the mangled body lay naked on the tracks. His right leg was torn from the body, his left limb crushed, his head divided near the eyes, his trunk so torn as to permit the entrails to escape." A witness earlier that day said that Knecht was intoxicated as he walked down the tracks toward Akron to stay with his brother. Knecht left a wife, three young children and an elderly mother.

A stalled car across a railroad track was no contest for a locomotive in 1938. An elderly couple and their eleven-year-old granddaughter, Betty Miller, of Shelhart Road in Loyal Oak, were all killed. One of the helpless individuals was carried 500 feet down the tracks. The engineer sounded his whistle and ground the brakes as the car entered the tracks at Route 21, scattering the car 1,500 feet until the train came to a stop. The grandfather, Hurl Perry, was hurled through the air 50 feet, and the little girl's body fell along the railway. The grandmother, Ina Bell, was found 500 feet from the crossing and near the car.

A brand-new limousine was no match for a roaring Erie Freight train in 1948. Blanche Obney, sixty-eight, of Barberton was killed, and her daughters, Mrs. Carl Hahn, thirty-one, of Barberton and Mrs. Dawn Bradchaty, living

Train rams limousine—one dead, two hurt. Akron Beacon Journal, *Newspapers.com*.

in Norton, were severely injured. The new funeral limousine was being pushed by the trio off of the railway after it had stalled at the Springfield Road and Barberton crossing. The ladies were on an outing to shop in Akron. Also in the vehicle was five-year-old Mary Ann, the daughter of Mrs. Hahn. She was taken afterward to the home of relatives and given a sedative.

Two Loyal Oak truck drivers witnessed the scene and reported to Patrolman Joseph Mollric and the *Akron Beacon Journal* this story: "We saw the lights and heard the whistle of the approaching train. At the same time, we saw the women trying to push the stalled car off the tracks. We started to help them but realized there was not time. Mrs. Obney heard us and started to run so did the others but it was too late. The engine struck the car broadside and hurtled it into the women. They were scattered like tenpins."

The owner of the demolished limousine, Hahn Funeral Home, was called to respond with an ambulance as well as other local funeral homes. The Hahn ambulance did not come, as it had a dead battery. Mr. Carl Hahn then did not have to witness the dead body of his beloved wife.

John Timothy, seventeen, was severely injured, and Richard McHenry, eighteen, and John Leppzer, sixteen, were killed in a 1928 vehicle accident that involved an Erie Freight Train in Norton Center. Deputy Sheriff J.R. Butcher, who investigated the crash, reported that there were skid marks on the pavement and that Timothy was the driver. The car had left the pavement, veering into a nearby ditch then back onto the tracks.

Falling asleep along a rail line in New Portage was probably not one of Ralph Wilson's better decisions. In 1902, Wilson fell asleep, rolled over and threw his arms above his head and across the tracks. Along came a train, which cut off both of his hands.

Grieving children, Grace, nine, and Arthur, sixteen, were notified of the death of both of their parents. Charles L. Blakeslee, fifty-eight, and Clara E. Blakeslee, forty-three, who were killed due to a train-car accident at Norton Center. In October 1926, the Blakeslees were on their way to Medina from Dover when they were struck by an Erie locomotive. Charles's body was dragged one hundred feet.

PLANES

Plunging to the ground in a nosedive in front of Lena Smith's home in Sherman in 1940 was a two-passenger plane flown by Robert Days of Copley. Days escaped with only scratches, but his companion, Ray E. Hutchinson, twenty-four, spent the next few days afterward fighting for his life in an area hospital.

Gasoline from the full tanks dumped onto the ground all around the plane and close to Smith's home. The plane's ignition was still on when sheriff's deputies arrived. It was a wonder that Smith's house did not go up in flames and that both men were not trapped inside the plane to die an ugly death.

The cause of the crash was determined to be when Days went into a power stall just one hundred feet off the land. Without a chance to come out of the dive, the plane crashed. Hutchinson had terrible cuts to his head and face and part of the plane went through his left eye. He also suffered a skull fracture, and both of his legs were broken. Unable to overcome so many injuries, Hutchinson passed away days later. He was married and had a son.

If only to become a pilot, Chester Boley, thirty, was in air training outside of his job as a tire builder for B.F. Goodrich in 1941. Eager to get his pilot's license, Boley started his flying instructions at the Ling Field in Sherman. Just after taking off, his plane crashed. The aircraft climbed rapidly and steep, made a downward turn, went into a spin and fell into a stand of trees near the airport. Two hours later, Boley was pronounced dead at Barberton Citizen's Hospital from internal injuries and a fractured skull.

The late Virginia Knox Swain told the author that she remembered her father, Fred Swain, telling her about a small plane that crashed on their farm in 1938. She recalls him telling her that a body came crashing through the windshield. Two young Barberton men died in the crash, coming down due to a defective aileron. The dead were Thomas J. Stuver, twenty-three and Charles Duncan, twenty-four.

Engine trouble was said to cause the demise of a blue and silver dual control plane with two occupants near Loyal Oak in 1950. The plane crashed into a field and broke into two pieces near Route 21 and ruptured into an inferno. Both of the occupants were charred beyond recognition. Dead were ex–air force pilot Fred Burk, thirty, and Edward Beals, both of Alliance.

In 1946, brothers Michael Strboya, twenty-six, and Robert Strboya, twenty-one, survived their plane crashing in a field on Reimer Road, near Loyal Oak. Taking off from Norton's only airport, Ling Field (also known as Barberton Airport and Sherman Field), the two were flying for four hours and ran out of gas. The pair crash-landed, causing Michael to suffer a skull fracture and Robert a terrible mouth laceration.

In 1946, two Sun Rubber employees went out for a joy ride from Ling Field without authorization. According to family members, both employees were said to have left for work in the morning just like any other day. Mary Watson, co-owner of the flying field said the couple, a man and a woman, showed up early in the morning. George M. Kling Jr. of Barberton and Gennesse June Fickle of Portage Lakes both died this ill-fated day in a

Top: Ray E. Hutchinson. *Bottom*: Chester Boley. Akron Beacon Journal, *Newspapers.com*.

Plane wreckage near the Barberton Airport. Akron Beacon Journal, *Newspapers.com*.

brand-new Aeronca Champion trainer tandem model. Observers shared how they had heard a roar as the plane flew over and was going at a great rate of speed and height. The plane crashed, spreading wreckage over one hundred feet on Nome Avenue in Copley. The bodies of the victims were crushed entirely and unrecognizable. Kling left behind a wondering wife as she had just packed his lunch that morning as he left for work. Fickle was a divorcée with two children. Sun Rubber officials said neither had reported for their 6:00 a.m. shift that day.

Top, left: Thomas J. Stuver. Akron Beacon Journal, *Newspapers.com.*

Top, right: Robert Strboya, who lost his teeth in a plane crash. Akron Beacon Journal, *Newspapers.com.*

Bottom: A curious crowd gathers around the plane wreckage where Tomas Stuver and Charles Duncan were found. Akron Beacon Journal, *Newspapers.com.*

Top: Mike Strboya. Akron Beacon Journal, *Newspapers.com.*

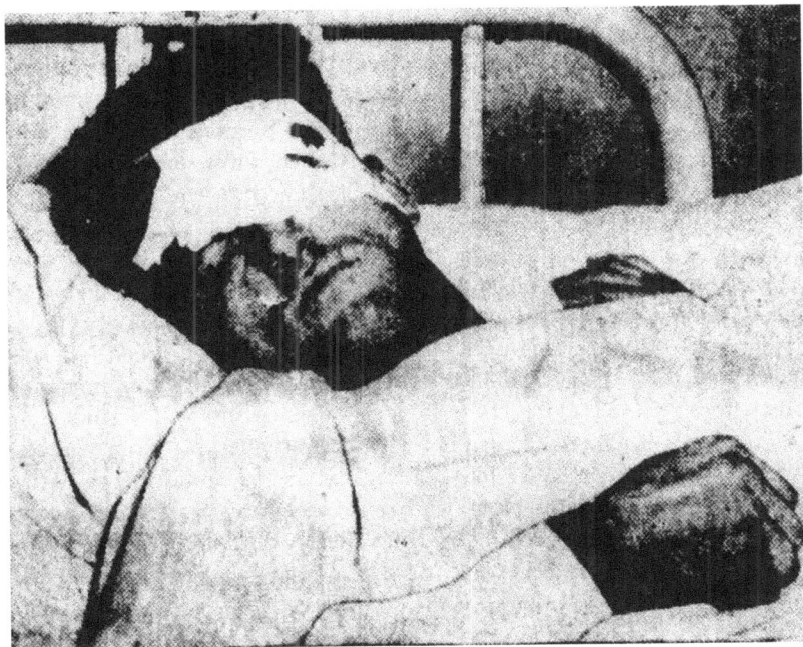

Bottom: Gennesse Fickle and George M. Kling shown next to the wreckage of the plane where they died. Akron Beacon Journal, *Newspapers.com.*

AUTOMOBILES

Soaring off Route 224 in 1937, one mile west of Norton Center, inside a stolen car were Loyal Oak resident Frederick J. Gordon, twenty-two, and the driver, Jack Cheshire of Akron, who denied any wrongdoing. When Cheshire was told of the death of Gordon, he showed no emotion. Gordon's body was found in the back seat of the bloody wrecked car.

Crashing into a tractor trailer in Loyal Oak caused the death of four North Carolina men on their way home from Easter holiday. Killed were James Wilson, eighteen; Henry Wilson, twenty-one; Charles W. Henson, eighteen; and Cecil Perkins, twenty-three. Letters found in the men's pockets led investigators to the opinion that they were headed home from Easter break from their jobs at the Fisher Body Company plant in Cleveland.

The driver of a tractor trailer, Leroy Paine, thirty-five, of Akron, claimed that he had the green light while heading east on 261 on his way to Akron when the car smashed into his trailer. Fog was in the area at the time, and the 1944 Club Coupe had its top sheared off while the rear wheels on the tractor trailer were gone. This 1953 scene was said to be one of the most horrifying that sheriff's deputies had ever seen.

In 1957, suits were filed in common pleas court, charging that the tractor trailer being driven east on Route 261 went through a red light. The estate of Cecil Perkins and James and Harry Wilson both sought damages of $100,000 each. The Hensons filed for $200,000. The jury of seven men and five women reported to Judge Thomas M. Powers for or against Commercial Motor Freight Company of Case Avenue in Akron. Arguing the case over who had the green light was attorney Charles M. Scanlon for the plaintiff and William A. Kelly for the defense. By 1958, a $40,000 verdict came in and was awarded to Mildred Perkins, wife of Cecil Perkins and mother of two girls ages six and seven.

In 1953, after visiting at a hospital with their son Jay, four, who had been struck by a car earlier in the day, parents Dwight Huff, thirty-eight, and Faye Huff and other car passengers were not aware of the fate that awaited them the next day at an intersection in Loyal Oak. Violet Huff, thirty-nine, sister of Dwight, and friend Roberta Adams, twenty-six, who was driving in this 1953 accident were to have their own life upended by a car accident. Dead were Dwight Huff and Roberta Adams. Huff's wife, Faye, was badly injured, and Huff's sister Violet later died. Living as a woman, the coroner discovered that Adams was actually a man and was the driver who crashed through a red light and struck a northbound truck and another car.

Twisted metal and broken bodies are all that was left of four young men killed in a traffic accident on Easter break. Akron Beacon Journal, *Newspapers.com*.

Eyewitness accounts say that the truck ran the stoplight. A sad ending to this tragic tale is that four-year-old Jay Huff also died that day.

Being classified as 1-A by the draft board might have saved Bernard Carberry from landing in the pen for causing the death of three women in a horrendous car-truck crash in Loyal Oak. In April 1943, Carberry of Uhrichsville was driving a truck full of coal, went through a red light and crashed into a car carrying Linnie Marie Murphy, twenty-four; Maude Meager, fifty; and Florence Deisz. Having to meet the military requirement to pass a physical exam would dismiss Carberry of charges so that he could enter the armed service. Carberry's downfall was due to a technical legal question brought by his legal counsel in a past indictment against him. Carberry was charged with six counts of manslaughter in the second degree.

Joe Hooser, a Norton Township high school junior, was killed in 1957 when the car he was driving was hit head-on by another auto. Bryan Walton,

THIS TRUCK AND CAR IN THE FATAL LOYAL OAK CRASH PILED UP AT BOWER'S GENERAL STORE

A car versus truck accident in Loyal Oak that took the lives of two people. Akron Beacon Journal, *Newspapers.com.*

Clockwise from top left: Joe Hocser Norton Township junior killed in a 1957 car accident. Akron Beacon Journal, *Newspapers.com*; Charles Tomblin. Akron Beacon Journal, *Newspapers.com*; Martin J. McCumsey. Akron Beacon Journal, *Newspapers.com*; Laburn Lydic died after slamming head-on into a utility pole while driving his car. *NHS yearbook.*

Car driven by Charles Tomblin, who was the thirtieth traffic fatality in Summit County in 1954. Akron Beacon Journal, *Newspapers.com.*

forty-six, of Barberton was trying to pass another vehicle on Barber Road at about 9:30 p.m. Walton said that he didn't see Hooser's car until it was too late, and he did try to veer away unsuccessfully. Walton had three passengers, who were all injured.

Charles Tomblin, twenty-nine, the father of three children, died in a car crash, and his brother, twenty-one-year-old Donald, was listed in fair condition at an Akron City Hospital in 1954. The Tomblin brothers grew up on Clarks Mill Road in Norton. The older Tomblin, who was driving, was trying to pass a northbound truck on Cleveland-Massillon Road (Old 21), just past Shellhart Road, when he hit a culvert, which caused the car to ram through four mailboxes and hurl the pair into the windshield. Charles Tomblin was an employee with the Seiberling Rubber Company and was a World War II army veteran.

Laburn Lydic, twenty-two, of Cleveland-Massillon Road had spent part of the night at an all-night truck stop restaurant on Norton Avenue in 1954, leaving about 4:30 a.m. and heading east toward Norton Center. The roadway was slick from falling rain, and he lost control of his car as it skidded down Norton Avenue near Long Drive. He traveled 180 feet left of center, careened off the roadway and slammed head-on into a utility pole, cutting it completely in half.

Tearing off the front end and wheels of a car and then traveling two hundred feet and hitting a mailbox post was a bad start to the day for five Barberton High School students and especially for Ethel M. Wike. Fifty-five-year-old Wike of Hametown Road was killed when her car was hit by a car driven by Frank Peison, seventeen. Peison's car with his four passengers went left of center while traveling at a high speed westbound on Wooster Road and hit Wike's car head-on. The five boys were trying out a car that they had been working on in their high school mechanics class in 1975.

In August 1927, a misplaced road sign might have been the cause of an accident that killed Martin J. McCumsey, a foreman for B.F. Goodrich. The road that McCumsey and his companion, H.M. Berry, a coworker, were traveling on was actually closed, but the sign that gave the warning looked as though it was for another side street. Because there was no barrier or any cautionary signs except for the misleading sign, it was easy to make the mistake of continuing on the Loyal Oak Road, known today as Akron-Wadsworth Road, 261, as it was being widened. As the two men were headed down a hill, they came upon a cement mixer with no lights, and without time to react, the car crashed into the mixer, overturned three times and was completely destroyed. Berry escaped injury and crawled from the wreck and was able to make it to a nearby home to seek help. McCumsey died of his injuries.

A joy ride to Pittsburgh, Pennsylvania, ended with tragedy for Earl Riley, forty, of Akron, a father of six, the children's ages ranging from seven to fourteen. Riley, a bird enthusiast, was headed to Pittsburgh on a Friday night at 11:00 p.m. to obtain more birds for his collection. A welder at the Akron Transportation Company, Riley died as he was thrown into a ditch as his car pitched frightfully across an open field just east of Norton Center in 1936. There he struck a telephone pole and skidded another 125 feet. Riley's body was found in the ditch at the point where the car left the road.

Paula Gaynor called her husband, Donn, at 1:00 p.m. at the *Beacon Journal*, where he was employed, to tell him that she was taking their granddaughter Cynthia to the doctor for a cut on her chin. Cynthia had fallen, and her mother didn't think it was serious, but she might need stitches. By 2:30 p.m.,

Clockwise from top left: Earl Riley; Paula Gaynor; Patricia Wines; Cynthia Loree Wines. Akron Beacon Journal, *Newspapers.com.*

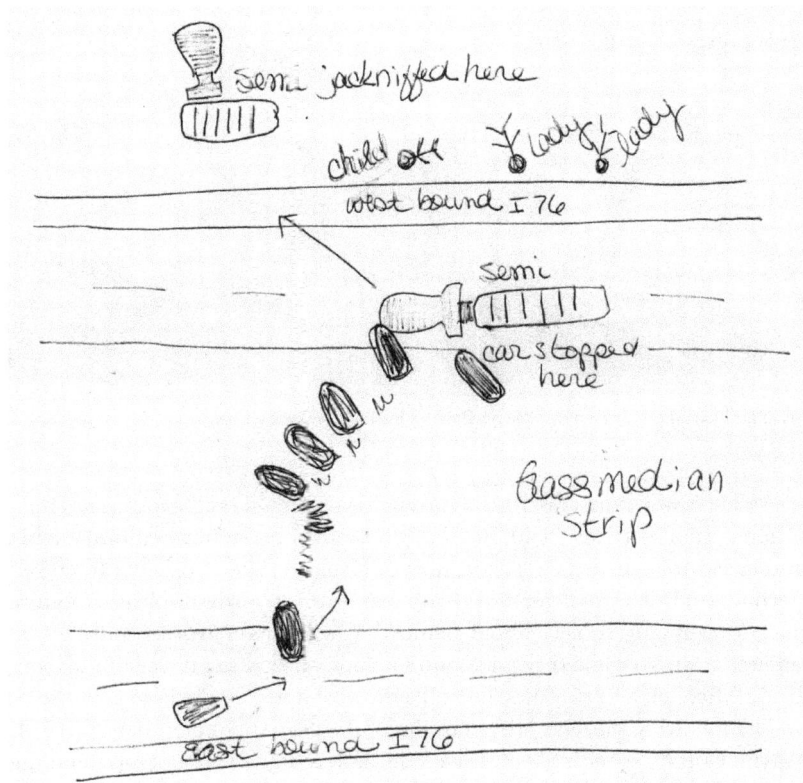

Diagram of the accident, with Gaynor and Wines drawing by the author, taken from police sketch. Akron Beacon Journal, *Newspapers.com.*

Donn Gaynor received another call informing him that his wife had been in a car accident that he needed to go to the Barberton Citizens Hospital. In an instant, in 1974, three generations of a Norton family were swept away. All three occupants of the car driven by Paula were thrown from the vehicle, a 1963 two-door Pontiac, landing on the berm on the north side of the road when it hit a tractor trailer head-on. Killed were Paula "Joan" Gaynor, forty-three; Patricia Wines, nineteen, daughter of Paula and Donn; and their granddaughter Cynthia Loree Wines, two. The car carrying the ladies careened across the median as it was traveling east just past the Cleveland-Massillon Road overpass where it smashed into the front left side of a westbound tractor trailer. After the car crashed into the truck,

Semi and car in the aftermath. Akron Beacon Journal, *Newspapers.com.*

the semi plowed into a ditch, and the engine ended up on the highway. Paula suffered injuries to her head, including a brain contusion, a cerebral edema and lacerations of the scalp face, liver and spleen. She also had a fractured sternum and ribs. The cause of death was listed as cardiorespiratory failure due to traumatic subarachnoid hemorrhage. In other words, sadly, Paula suffered a stroke while driving. Donn Gaynor was left to grieve with his son, Donn Michael, and two daughters, Paula Mae and Pamela Jane.

The following piece appeared in the *Norton Pride* on September 26, 1974. Wayne County schools always gave their kids a day off school to attend the Wayne County Fair. On September 9, Bill Totten and four of his closest friends set out for this adventure. His best friend, Charlie Hatfield, was driving, and Bill was in the back seat. Suddenly a tire rim from a newly mounted tire let loose, and the car proceeded to flip end over end and then rolled sideways five times. A truck driver behind them immediately called for help. Bill's head hit the roof on the first flip, and his neck was broken. No one else was seriously injured. Bill spent the next ten days in traction at Children's Hospital, conscious but paralyzed. His mother, Helen Totten, related: "A ray of hope came the day he raised his hand and said 'Hi,' he was really great, he never blamed anyone." Bill, seventeen, liked to fix old bikes and to ride horseback. His diploma was handed to his mom at his funeral.

Three of nine teenagers on their way home from a church hayride were in serious condition after a car accident on Silver Creek Road in Wadsworth. Listed as serious and in the Barberton Citizens Hospital ICU were Philip Ault, eighteen; his sister, Barbara Ault, fifteen; and Julia Harn, fifteen, all of

Nine teenagers were in this speeding station wagon driven by Philip Ault. His sister died as a result of the accident. Akron Beacon Journal, *Newspapers.com.*

Barberton. Listed in fair condition was Linda Hicks, fourteen, of Norton. Two others who were listed in satisfactory condition were taken to Wadsworth Hospital. They were Diane Meeker, thirteen, and Paul F. Goff, fifteen.

Speeding recklessly down Silver Creek Road at about 9:20 p.m., the Chrysler station wagon driven by Philip Ault and loaded with the youths vaulted across a set of railroad tracks and careened into the air. As the full car of young people landed, it tore off a fence, bounced off of a steel girder and slammed into a steam shovel where city sewer construction had been taking place.

The accident took place on September 11, 1977, and on September 18, Philip Ault's sister Barbara died from her injuries. She was a sophomore at Barberton High School. In October 1980, after a two-week trial, a verdict was reached by the Summit County Common Pleas Court to award Linda Hicks, then seventeen, one of the passengers, $250,000.

A lawsuit was filed against Kokosing Construction Company of Frederickstown, the City of Wadsworth and Consolidated Rail Corporation by Wayne Ault, the father of Philip and Barbara. Ault was seeking $400,000 for his daughter's death and claimed the companies listed were all negligent. His suit was dismissed along with others who sued for compensation. Ms.

Hicks had also sued the church group and the church in Barberton who sponsored the hayride, Moore Memorial Methodist Church.

On a side note, the author was invited to go on this evening adventure but had declined knowing the driving habits of the driver of the Chrysler station wagon.

MANGLED MASSES

On their way home from a local carnival and having gone roller skating, the night ended badly for a pair of teenagers in 1940. A hit skip motorist took the life of sixteen-year-old Harold Clark of Barberton and broke the leg of fourteen-year-old Margaret Dubel as they walked home on their very first date.

Margaret Dubel, fourteen, and Harold Clark, sixteen, on their first date when tragedy struck. Akron Beacon Journal, *Newspapers.com.*

Evidence to convict the skipper included paint chips from the coat of Dubel and eyewitness accounts. The car had bits of hair on the windshield, concluding that Clark had been hurtled onto the hood of the vehicle.

Turning to attorney Fred Smoyer, twenty-year-old Harlold A. Freidt, an insurance agent, spent a wakeful night before he surrendered to his deed. Smoyer took Freidt to Alva Russell, a prosecutor, and to Judge Charles Kelly, who waived a preliminary hearing, which angered the sheriff's department who were working to solve the case. Out on $1,500 bond, Freidt admitted that he was passing another vehicle when he suddenly saw something, hit it and just kept going.

A new barn being built on the farm of Jacob Boerstler, south of Loyal Oak, caused many men helping their neighbor to perish or be badly injured. Between seventy-five and one hundred men showed up for the barn raising as the women folk were busily in charge of feeding the many hard-working volunteers. The frame of the barn was being raised by the numerous men when the side posts slipped, and the logs fell onto fifty workers lifting with pike poles.

Pools of blood and loud moans met the mob of women who descended on the scene, many of whom fainted at the sight. Many men were pinned, others were unconscious and some were crushed and had their backs split in half. Frank Ehrich's chest was crushed, and Andrew Lahr was bruised and cut. Joseph Reimer had his back injured, and men were hurled to the foundation while some had been knocked to the floor below. Milton Boerstler had his shoulder blade dislocated and had internal injuries. William Bauer had a nasty slash on his head and neck. Joseph Bauer had a serious injury to his spine while George Hoffman endured a leg injury. Eugene wise was cut and bruised, as was Aaron Betz and Daniel Snyder, who had internal injuries. Jacob Kurtz, Frank Ehrich and Milton Boerstler were all said to have passed away from their injuries.

Jacob Boerstler, still working his farm years later, succumbed to a heat stroke and died at the age of sixty-six, leaving a wife and six children.

The following story of mangled masses is a true story of horror and sorrow in the Norton community and especially for two young Norton children.

A clinical psychologist testified on behalf of two children ages ten and eight that an accident taking both of their parents' lives caused "loss of all security systems," according to the *Akron Beacon Journal*, and "traumatic shock." On March 20, 1979, Reverend John D. Barrickman Sr. and his wife, Patricia Barrickman, of Norton were both killed when a 140-foot slab of concrete weighing fifteen to twenty tons fell onto their car. The Barrickmans

were traveling east on Interstate 76 through Akron when the walkway of the Grant Street bridge, currently under construction, fell onto their car, completely cutting it in half. Falling rubble also hit a truck, injuring two riders. Kenneth J. Hinson, forty-eight, and Alton Gray of Roy Stone Transportation Corporation out of Martinsville, Virginia, were flipped in their truck onto its cap. Hinson sustained a broken shoulder and other injuries while Gray suffered from broken toes. The Barrickmans were transported by ambulance to Akron City Hospital, where they were both pronounced DOA (dead on arrival). The cause of death listed for Mrs. Barrickman was cardiorespiratory failure due to avulsion of the brain. Mr. Barrickman died due to cardiorespiratory failure due to a crushed skull. Details of the autopsy report that Mrs. Barrickman suffered from a massive crush injury with the absence of brain tissue, four dorsal fractures and a complete transection of the spinal cord. It also included the laceration of the aorta, liver and spleen with multiple fractures of the humerus, ulna, radius and hands. Mr. Barrickman had a lacerated heart, liver, lungs, diaphragm, spleen and adrenals. His spine was completely cut in half with multiple fractures of the skull and maceration of the brain.

The Barrickmans were described by the community as loving, giving and generous and all-around great people. Reverend Barrickman had started a church in 1975 called the Bible Temple of God in Barberton. He started

Opposite, left: Reverend John Barrickman. Akron Beacon Journal, *Newspapers.com.*

Opposite, right: Patricia Barrickman. Akron Beacon Journal, *Newspapers.com.*

Right: State, city and construction officials view the concrete chunk that fell onto the Barrickmans' car, cutting it in half and killing both occupants. Akron Beacon Journal, *Newspapers.com.*

Below: The Barrickmans' car split in two. Akron Beacon Journal, *Newspapers.com.*

with a handful of members in his congregation, and it grew to eighty-five members in a short time.

Numerous officials, including local city engineers, ODOT (Ohio Department of Transportation) bridge inspectors from the Federal Highway Administration and an insurance representative, came onto the scene to access the situation. City of Akron supervisors were on the site when the bridge was under construction, and the bridge had been inspected three months prior. At the point in which the bridge was being constructed, it was not considered a requirement for scaffolds to be placed underneath to catch falling scrap.

A committee of five members of both state transportation and state construction experts came together to do an investigation and a study. A more extensive study was also to take place later at the cost of $25,000 to the state. This was to be done by a Pennsylvania firm by the name of Modjeski and Masters.

Meanwhile, the brother-in-law of Patricia Barrickman, Emlous Lattea, filed suit in the Common Pleas Court of Summit County. The suit charged that the John J. Ruhlin Construction Company, the City of Akron, the State of Ohio and the National Engineering and Construction Company in Strongsville should be held accountable. The charges were that they all unsuccessfully provided protection to the public by not using protective devices or closing the expressway while bridge work was being done. It also charged negligence in the bridge repair by not following proper engineering protocol.

In court proceedings, discussion of reports on the bridge were made public. It was deemed that the disclosure could prejudice the conclusion of the filed $10 million suit. There was some confusion about the cutting of metal rods that were to reinforce the inside of the concrete walkway. State and city inspectors were on hand while this work was being done. The particular rods that were being cut would not necessarily have caused any danger, but it was learned later that a second row of reinforcing rods did not exist inside the structure. These rods might have kept the entire block of concrete from falling onto the highway below.

Almost a year later, it was determined in reports relayed by the Ohio Transportation director, David L. Weir, that in fact the cutting of the reinforcing rods without careful plans was the cause of the span collapsing. William B. Ruhlin, president of Ruhlin Construction, the company doing the actual bridge work, said that the sidewalk would not have fallen if the lower set of reinforcement rods had been in the slab as noted in the primary plans. He also noted that the Ruhlin Company had done a comparable job on the other side of the same bridge where the lower rods were in place, so it was common sense to expect the same on both sides.

As the case moved on, by June 1981, the Ruhlin Company and the City of Akron both admitted to negligence in the case. The next phase of court proceedings with the Ohio Court of Claims in Columbus was to determine how much in compensation the relatives of the Barrickmans would be granted.

Pending during all of the commotion was a case of *Ruhlin v. the City of Akron*. No one entity wanted to take responsibility, so they pitted themselves one against the other. The city felt that it was not liable because the state oversaw the task. And the city inspectors were under contract with the state.

Going back to the children of the Barrickmans, Dr. Robert O. Kirkhart testified to the court expressing how they were fairing under these circumstances. Along with the shock, Kimberly Barrickman had anxiousness and John Barrickman seemed to be infuriated and was afraid to leave home. He could not function on his tasks at school given this horrendous and tragic time. The children both testified in court.

Another consideration in the case was the Barrickmans' niece Terri Harvey, fifteen, who survived an automobile accident in 1972. Harvey lost her parents and two siblings in the mishap. Her grandparents, Patricia Barrickman's parents, Mr. and Mrs. Olen Harvey, took care of the girl, who was left brain damaged. When the grandparents passed away, the Barrickmans were to become her guardians. Donna Lattea, Mrs. Barrickmans sister, and brother-in-law Emlous became the guardians of the Barrickman children.

The trial took place with six women and two men. There was a broad difference in the amount that the prosecutor wanted for the family compared to the defense. Considered one of the largest monetary verdicts in the court's history, the family of Patricia and Reverend John Barrickman Sr. were awarded a total of $1 million. The verdict was returned against John G. Ruhlin Construction Company and the City of Akron. The question still remained though, who would pay what portion of the $1 million.

The trial lasted four days, and the jury deliberated for two and a half hours. An interesting fact that had been left out to the jurors was how the bridge collapse actually happened. This fact was left out because both parties on trial had admitted to negligence. After the trial, some of the jurors, finding out about the cause, said that they might have awarded more money to the family. The family of the Barrickmans seemed to be pleased with the outcome, with jurors saying that both the prosecution and the defense did an excellent job.

With the verdict in, the Ruhlin Company and the city were still at odds. Why did the city and the state not have to pay anything and the Ruhlin

Company foot the entire bill? The Ruhlin Company wanted compensation by both parties. Assistant Attorney General Robert S. Tongren weighed in by saying, according to the *Akron Beacon Journal*, "It's clear Ruhlin and Ruhlin alone had control over demolition of the bridge. The circle of arguments will never end as Ruhlin still contends that the lower rods were cut without their knowledge. But the fact remains, two innocent individuals lost their lives on March 20, 1979 leaving behind a grieving family."

The story of Jacob Flickinger of Loyal Oak has a sad ending, which affected not only a wife but also thirteen children. Flickinger was a blacksmith hailing from hearty Swiss stock when his grandfather came to the area in 1763. Flickinger learned the trade of blacksmithing from his soon to be father-in-law, Isaac Weyrick, in 1874. Flickinger married Sarah Editha Weyrick, and to this day, the tiny home where they raised their family still stands.

Jacob and Editha celebrated their golden wedding anniversary in 1924. A lavish spread was put on for their thirteen children, along with forty-five grandchildren and a great grandchild. But just one week later, tragedy struck when Jacob was hit in the back by a vehicle in front of his home, which killed him.

Tragedy in the family had struck earlier when Editha and Jacob's son Charles, eleven, was run over by a train and lost his leg. The poor lad got an infected pus-filled arm that had to be amputated. This procedure took place in the family living room while mother sat in another room praying as she listened to the sound of flesh and bone being carved away. Jacob and a neighbor wrapped the limb in newspaper and took it to the Loyal Oak Cider Mill. Both hesitated to throw the appendage into the fire there. A willing customer took charge and did the deed.

3

BLAZES AND WATER

Blazes

According to the *Akron Beacon Journal*, in December 1895, "Hungry flames swept down a large barn and at the same time burned to a crisp the body of a young man who was attempting to rescue his team of horses. In one of the mangers a charred mass was found. The flesh on what remained of the body was roasted and the skull was glowing hot. Several buckets of water were poured upon the remains and the skull fell into pieces allowing the brains to fall upon the ground. Both legs had been burned off at the knee and both arms at the elbow."

The twenty-five-year-old man who burned was Oliver F. Baughman of Sherman. Baughman was helping his brother-in-law William Hackenberg by moving hay from a barn in Western Star to a farm owned by George Bird in Sherman.

Ten-year-old Eddie Thomas held a lantern in the hay mow as it was getting dark outside. Thomas accidentally fell, and the lantern set a large blaze. Both Baughman and Hackenberg jumped into action to free the horses inside the barn. Hackenberg and a few horses made it out of the barn, but Baughman was missing.

Baughman was an only child, so delivering the news to Baughman's parents was a grim task. Mother and father were overcome with grief, with father groaning in his hands and mother sobbing and crying for her son.

Left: Connie. Akron Beacon Journal, *Newspapers.com.*

Right: Fire levels Ling Airport. Akron Beacon Journal, *Newspapers.com.*

In 1938, a barn fire at the homestead of Charles H. Lahr was said to be seen ten miles away and drew in observers from nearby towns and stopped traffic. The barn, located in Norton Center, was built by Lahr's grandfather, who had come to Norton in a covered wagon from Pennsylvania. It was a total loss.

In 1953, Connie Ellis, seven, of Oak Road died from burns she suffered after her curiosity for candles and matches got the best of her. Somehow, Ellis's clothing had caught on fire, and a sister heard her call coming from the yard.

Lightning was the cause of $70,000 in damage in July 1948 at Ling Field in Sherman. A total loss, the airport listed a restaurant, control tower, hangar, seven planes, club rooms and an administration building, all gone.

Gasoline tanks were blowing up and a forty-gallon vat of airplane fiber glass exploded. Fire departments from four agencies came to battle the blaze. Mary Watkins, the assisting manager, was able to rescue files and records.

On his stomach and elbows and almost unconscious, Richard Spigelmyer, eleven, crawled to the door of his home after being burned badly. Spigelmyers legs, hands and clothing had caught fire while pouring kerosene over open coals, causing an explosion in 1940.

WATER

In 1881, the eleven-year-old son of Rueben and Elizabeth Stauffer died. Known as "Bertie," Milton A. Stauffer made his way down Clark's Mill Road and drowned in the overflowing Wolf Creek, one of the many streams crossing through the township.

Tangled in weeds and found by a rowing party in New Portage in 1890 was the body of a newborn baby. The body was facedown and naked. According to physician C.W. Whipple the white male of seven and a half pounds was only twenty-four hours old and born alive. The theory was that someone had driven to the town and thrown the child off a nearby bridge.

In May 1893, a brave man faced imminent danger, as he was the only one to make the decision to help a young lad. Risking his own life in Botzum at the Cuyahoga River was Grant Furry, who was the station agent of the Valley Railway. The Cuyahoga River was severely swollen with springtime rains to the point of swamping a local road and bridge. It was deemed impassable at the time, as it was at least six to seven feet deep. One man named Weber and his fourteen-year-old son from Clark's Mill in Norton thought they could make it across in a wagon with a double team. The entire team, wagon, Weber and son were swept away by the raging current. Weber was able to catch the horses and cut the traces and managed to get to dry land. The wagon seat where the boy was riding came off the wheels and headed down a watery path. The boy was finally pinned against a tree and was in danger of being crushed or drowned, and the only way to reach him would have been to jump in the water and float to him. By lashing himself with ropes, Furry took on the task of floating to the boy and dismantling him from his position. Other men took to the ropes and pulled them to safety. Furry was said to have many cuts from the barbed wire that ran under the current.

The only thing visible was a small straw hat floating on the water in an old well in Norton. Vernon Waldron, two, wandered off and fell to his death and drowned in 1915.

Leaving behind a widow and nine children in 1932, fifty-seven-year-old Jerry Diefendorff of Norton Center fell into his water well and drowned while drawing water. Years later, his

Milton "Bertie" Stauffer. *Author photograph.*

twenty-seven-year-old son, Jerry D. Diefendorf, suffered the same fate. He was not a swimmer and was last seen floating on a raft; he was found at the bottom of an unattended swimming pool at a friend's home.

Trying to retrieve a dropped orange was the cause of the accidental drowning of nineteen-month-old Bradley Wilson in 1948. The child was found face down in a drainage ditch on Hemphill Road.

While swimming at Lake Anna in Barberton in 1955, Thomas J. Mong, nine, of Weber Drive wasn't missed all day until his ride showed up to take him home. Finally found by a chain of boys wading in waist-deep water, they stumbled upon the body.

Left-behind clothing and a purse were the only clues that Alice Underwood, twenty-nine, of Coventry Township and Roy Saunders, thirty-one, of Franklin Township had been swimming in a local abandoned sand pit in Norton. Both were seen skinny dipping late in the evening. After Underwood's boyfriend reported her missing, divers from Copley, Bath and Cuyahoga Falls were called in to search for the pair. Both were found in about fifteen feet of water on this weed-choked pond off Clark's Mill Road.

In 1975, nineteen-year-old James F. Parks's body was recovered from a local Norton Pond. He and some of his buddies were taking a dip in the pond behind Hope United Methodist Church on Hametown Road, which was on the farmland of David B. Anderson. At this same location in 1955, nine-year-old Clyde Hughes, who could not swim, drowned while two of his companions tried desperately to save his life. Hughes, an only child and fourth grader at Loyal Oak School, along with his friends, was walking along the pond when Clyde fell in.

In June 1988, after Freda Hopkins dropped off her child with relatives on Johnson Road, Michael Hopkins, three, wandered away and drowned in a neighbor's pool. Freda Hopkins, twenty-four, was in Akron Municipal Court testifying against her common law husband, Joe Hopkins, thirty-

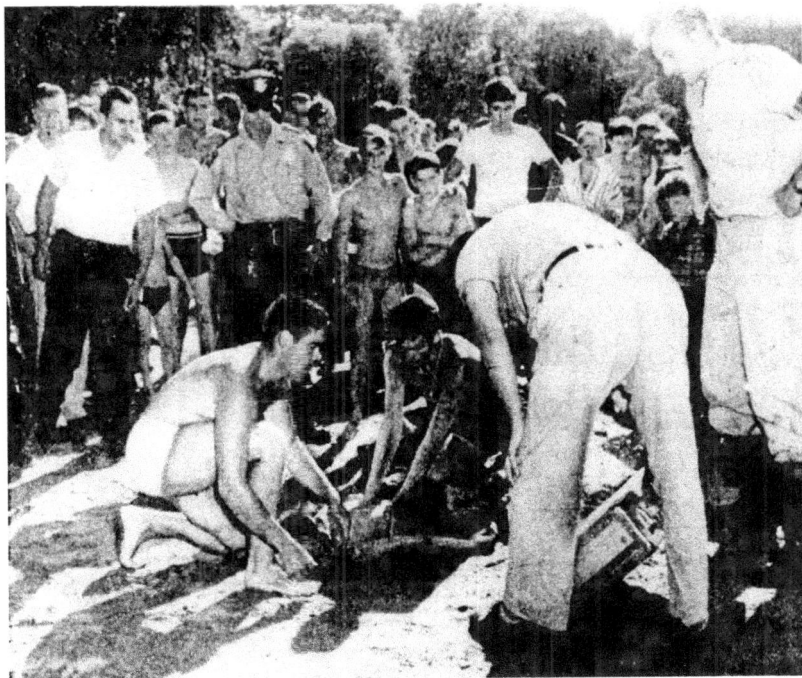

Opposite: Nineteen-month-old Bradley Wilson drowned in a drainage ditch. Akron Beacon Journal, *Newspapers.com*.

Above: Nine-year-old Tom Mong drowns in Lake Anna. Akron Beacon Journal, *Newspapers.com*.

Right: Tom Mong. Akron Beacon Journal, *Newspapers.com*.

three, who was also her uncle. Joe Hopkins was accused of beating their three-month-old daughter because she would not stop crying, leaving her in critical condition. Joe Hopkins punched the little girl in the abdomen, broke her wrist and nine ribs and the child also suffered from head injuries.

It was a case of confusion concerning Michael, as the relative on Johnson Road thought he was outside playing with her own children. The children had assumed that Michael was inside. A search ensued, and the family eventually notified the police. At around two o'clock in the afternoon, the Norton paramedics were called and found the boy trapped under a solar cover in the four-foot-deep pool.

4

ON THE LIGHTER SIDE

I n 1899, Ray Long had been spending time in the county jail with a charge of bastardy. He was let go on a $300 bond.

Items stolen from Oak Hettrick of Loyal Oak were destined for glory in the Wild West in 1909. Lewis Schlerdth, seventeen, had visions of becoming the second Buffalo Bill. He claimed that the West needed heroes to sweep the bloodthirsty "red man" from the plains. Schlerdth was a student of sensational writings. He hand rolled cigarettes with one hand the way his western heroes did. He didn't want to work on the family farm or go to school.

In the *Akron Beacon Journal*, we find this quote: "Lewis decided that the limits to life as it is lived in Loyal Oak were too circumscribed for a ready brave man who was willing to take his life in his hand and wade through gore, and he decided to go to the land of romance—the west."

Schlerdth needed an outfit fitting of his westward dreams, so he stole a repeating rifle, a Bowie knife, a revolver and cartridges and a belt. Late at night, he went to Hettrick's farm and knew just where to look. Only a mile from Loyal Oak he was apprehended by the constable, ruining any chance of making his way west and fighting the Indians or slaying a grizzly.

In 1926, Milton H. Miller, who lived on Wadsworth Road just west of Loyal Oak, reported over two hundred broilers were abducted from his farm

Stealing chickens got William L. Winters, twenty-two, shot by a shotgun and put into the county jail. Winters's wife accompanied him in the theft. The pair gained entrance to the coop through a window of A.D. Snyder's barn and were later charged with chicken stealing

Eighty skillet-sized fat hens were stolen from the Odom farm in Norton Center in 1936.

Poor Helen Brown, fifteen, of Shelhart Road got a zipper from her dress caught on her eyelid, and the harder her mom tried to unzip the zipper, the more the girl cried. Her mother finally cut away the fabric of the dress and left the entire zipper hanging from the girl's swelling eyelid as they dashed to the hospital. There a doctor used a janitor's tin snips to snip the offending object from the girl's lid. The doctor remarked that this was not an uncommon occurrence, since the hook-less fashion came about. Dr. Wellwood added that he treated mostly men for this predicament, and some had been very serious.

Barberton police had tried for at least ten years to catch the "skirt thief," also called the "petticoat thief." This thief loved to steal undergarments from clotheslines, especially ladies' silk undies. Starting around 1919, he gained entry through the back window of the home of J.M. Carter, 1010 Cornell Street, where he managed to escape with two petticoats. Barberton residents seemed amused by the stories, but some of the women were too humiliated to report any thefts of their delicates.

The home of Doctor O.A. Hille of Huron Street was targeted, with a silk petticoat being procured by the slick bandit. A pocketbook with money was left untouched. The bandit was on a mission for his items of femininity. At the house of Milo Sample, it was reported that a thief had broken in and

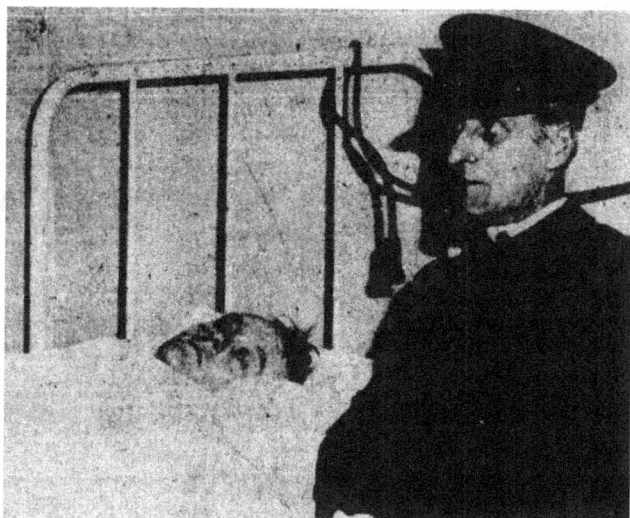

Henry Rice, forty-four, the "petticoat thief," with officer J.M. Head. *Akron Beacon Journal, Newspapers.com.*

stolen four petticoats and a silk nightgown. The home of Joseph H. Bauhart on Baird Avenue had been ransacked, but the thief was unable to obtain his prized possession, as the silks had been previously hidden by the residents. Stranger though was the fact that the Bauharts found a carefully folded silk dress lying on the bed. City Solicitor Ray E. Morton's home on Parker Avenue had been robbed numerous times. Silk under garments worth $300 came up missing. One of the favorite quarries was the trousseau of newly married ladies.

City administrators were fed up and embarrassed by the situation. So, a $1,000 reward was instituted "dead or alive" for the capture of the mysterious phantom. The city mayor, according to the *Barberton Herald*, offered to punish the captive by tying him or her to the flagpole at Lake Anna where the victims could have the chance to "let em have it by their own accord." After the reward was offered, the thief, with an accomplice, appeared to folks as they brazenly got away with petticoats in broad daylight.

By 1928, there was an arrest made of Henry Rice, forty-four, of Norton Center. Patrolman William Daugherty and Carl Obney set up surveillance at the home of Morton, feeling as though the marauder would make a return visit. They observed a man wandering in the vicinity of the Morton home and followed him. As the perpetrator ran, he was stopped by a bullet to his neck. He claimed to be innocent and in turn sued for damages of $50,700. He claimed that the right side of his head was paralyzed forever.

"Just a little walk in the park" from Bates Corners (Loyal Oak) through Wadsworth, Sharon, Copley, Bath and into Richfield in 1887 by the six-year-old daughter of Mr. and Mrs. Samuel Reimer was said to be twenty miles and lasted for days.

On her return from Richfield, according to the *Summit Beacon*, "demonstrations of rejoicing were very marked and enthusiastic indeed—the wonder on the one hand being that a young child could possibly have traveled so far in so short a time on her long and devious journey."

Fined $800 and chastised by Judge Fritch in 1926, David J. Jones of Hametown plead guilty to possessing whiskey. While his home was being raided, Jones's son ran away and busted a bottle that he was carrying. A man in the driveway, also with a bottle, smashed it against the house. Ten quarts of liquor were found stored in a special hiding place in the house. Jones insisted that he needed to bootleg for the money to take care of his seven kids. The judge wouldn't hear of it, saying it was just an excuse.

Three-year-old Bobby Joe Bloomer of Loyal Oak died from rabies in 1942 after being bitten on the eye and lip by a stray dog. The youngster was treated with fourteen inoculations of Pasteur injections but later passed away. What were his symptoms? It could be one of many, including paralysis, spasms, agitation, being aggressive and frothing at the mouth. It is considered a painful death. Eight of nine dogs tested after being captured in Summit County tested positive for symptoms of rabies. Dog bites were numbering from ten to twenty a day in Summit County, with the outbreak hitting the Loyal Oak area of Norton especially hard. In the early part of May 1942, people had reported dog bites to the county health director, Dr. E.R. Shaffer, and at least forty reports of stray dogs were included. Shaffer had given an order to keep dogs on their leash, stay at home and put in place a quarantine. The dog that bit young Bloomer was owned by a Barberton man and allowed his pet to run free. He admitted to knowing that the animal was sick. The dog was later put down eight miles from its home. The dog had also bitten other animals in the area, including other dogs, cats and even chickens. A bit of chaos ensued when Dr. Shaffer declared the situation grave in July. At the time, three suspected dogs whose heads tested positive for the virus proved that they had been infected with rabies. Many people in surrounding areas had reported being bitten and were ordered to get treatment. People were reportedly cruelly taking their pets out to the country and dropping them off.

Friends frantically searched high and low in 1920 for Willis. Willis had been badly injured in a car accident in the Norton Center area. Willis was speeding in his roadster on the wrong side of the road and crashed into a truck carrying livestock. The crash put the two drivers of the truck into the hospital, where they were both unresponsive. Others in the vicinity of the crash followed a trail of blood to locate Willis. Willis was not found, but more tragedy took place on the roadway. Two pigs lost their lives in the mishap. But on the good side, a bunch of surviving chickens made homes at area farms.

5

MISCELLANEOUS MAYHEM

For the second time in a few months, Henry Fortner's home had been dynamited by an unknown individual or individuals. Fortner, who in 1950 lived on Wadsworth Road, one and a half miles west of Loyal Oak, worked for B.F. Goodrich Company and was a union committee man of Local 5 United Rubber Workers, CIO and chairman of the local recreation committee. With $6,500 worth of damage to his home, he was sure someone was out to kill him, but who? One of the explosions occurred while Fortner was not at home, but relatives were there, including his wife, father-in-law and his two young nephews.

Fingers pointed toward forty-nine-year-old James Helton, a B.F. Goodrich employee, and his cohort Anthony Kinsinger, twenty-one. Kinsinger had admitted to being paid fifty dollars by Helton to bomb Fortner's home most recently in December of that year but not the earlier bombing that took place in April. Helton was said to have a beef with Fortner for being involved with his dismissal from the Goodrich Local 5.

Previously, Helton had said that Fortner had wanted the union to slow production at the plant and that union members who did not comply would be physically reprimanded. Helton had been beaten earlier on orders of union president George R. Bass. He had been called rude names and threatened at least thirty times and had found his toolbox full of spit and waste matter.

A court trial pitted Helton against Kinsinger. Helton denied being involved, and Kinsinger said that Helton had driven him to the Fortner home after they had been drinking over a period of hours. Feeling no fear now, they loaded

Above: Henry Fortner looks at damage to the foundation of his home after vandals set off dynamite. Akron Beacon Journal, *Newspapers.com.*

Opposite, top: James Helton and Anthony Kinsinger. Akron Beacon Journal, *Newspapers.com.*

Opposite, bottom: Mrs. Helton's body near Nimisila Reservoir. Akron Beacon Journal, *Newspapers.com.*

a cloth bag with dynamite, drove to the home, lit the fuse and threw the bag toward Fortner's home. The explosion cut a hole in the house base and a four-foot hole in the roof and shattered windows. Fortner's two nephews happened to be sleeping in the part of the house where the discharge was set but were not injured. Helton claimed that he had been drinking with a buddy until 3:00 a.m. at a club in Akron when the bombing happened.

After both Helton and Kinsinger were found guilty in a court trial in 1951, a new trial was wanted. Helton was facing one to seven years for malicious destruction and one to twenty years for illegal possession of dynamite. Helton

claimed that he was being framed. His conviction was upheld, and Helton was to serve two to seventeen years at the Ohio Penitentiary. Kinsinger, the star witness, had served nine months and got probation lasting five years.

Helton became a fugitive, skipping out of his $6,000 bond, and was being chased by his bondsman, Liborio "Whiskey Dick" Percoco, and Chief Deputy Ray Woodard of Summit County. Helton was traced through a series of five states and finally into Oklahoma, where he and his wife purchased a twenty-five-room hotel and Mr. Helton lived under the alias of James Moore.

As his pursuers were picking up on his trail, Helton took off again and this time headed west, moving to Roseburg, Oregon. Here he was captured because of a plan laid out by Percoco and Sheriff Woodard through a series of phone calls.

When Helton was arrested, he had a loaded shotgun in his possession, waiting for his chance to defend himself.

Flown back to Akron and again in the courtroom, Helton flared up and blamed the "Communists" of the Local 5 and denied being guilty. He said that the Communists kept him from the right to make a living. He said that he quit paying his dues to the Local 5 and got beaten for it and had been threatened to be fired. He also claimed that the sheriff and his deputies were holding his possessions and subjected him to abuse. He created havoc when his complaint continued that he wanted to remove the sheriff from office.

Meanwhile, in July 1954, Maude Helton, wife of James Helton, was found dead off Christman Road near the Nimisila Reservoir in the Portage Lakes area of Akron. Maude, a beautician, was found face down in the sand close to the reservoir. She had been missing for six months, but her son found her and brought her home to live with his dad.

The night that Maude disappeared, county detectives claimed that she had been drinking with a man and another couple. She and the unknown man went to Nimisila, a well-known place for lovers to hang out.

Mrs. Helton was known by the local authorities for previous charges stemming from disorderly conduct and intoxication. The cause of death was said to be from a brain hemorrhage due to a fall three weeks before, according to Coroner W.J. Pittenger.

Having served only a two-year sentence, Helton was released from prison, whereupon he found employment with Local 24 Teamsters Union and became a truck driver for All States Freight Incorporated. He was subsequently fired and sued the company for $24,000, claiming that the accidents that he had been in were because of bad weather. During his trial, union vice president George Allhouse had defended Helton, but the operations manager was not having it.

James Helton died of a sudden illness in 1976 at the age of seventy-five. Henry Fortner died in 1981 at the age of seventy-six.

By far one of the saddest tales and one still talked about in Norton was the death of two middle school boys who went missing on a cold and snowy February 18, 1979. A frantic search for Mark Holcomb, fourteen, and his friend John Erich, thirteen, was held in Loyal Oak after the boys were listed as missing while off looking for beer cans for their collections. They were known to search behind the Loyal Oak Car Wash, and a blood-sniffing dog twice led authorities to this location. The dog sat, which to them meant that the boys had possibly gotten into a vehicle there. Asked why the dog did not stop at the bin where the boys were subsequently found, the handler said that it was probably because of the number of people who had come and gone from that spot over and over looking for them, and the scent was not picked up.

John Ehrich

Over one hundred calls came pouring into the Norton Police Department and to the panicked families. Sightings of the boys came from as far away as Cleveland, Columbus and Akron. Psychics got involved and led the families and the police on wild goose chases. Every lead had to be followed no matter how small or strange.

Neither boy was considered a runaway. They were both good kids, according to the school district and their parents. They always phoned home if they were going to be late and always let their parents know where they were going. Along with the families and the

Mark Holcomb

John Ehrich and Mark Holcomb. Akron Beacon Journal, Newspapers.com.

police in a frenzied search was a helicopter crew from the National Guard. They flew low and searched every nook and cranny in a wide swath of land. One of the places they pinpointed was the Barberton Reservoir, where the boys were said to traverse on occasion. A psychic said that they saw a hole in the ice and that it had frozen over, that someone had put the boys in it. There was no indication of this. Also, since the reservoir is a source of drinking water, there was no fishing allowed, so there should have been no holes in the ice. Residents on snowmobiles and search parties were fanned out across the area. At one point, a metro bus driver insisted that he had picked up the boys and taken them to the local mall and then into Barberton. A woman

Collection container where Ehrich and Holcomb were found. Akron Beacon Journal, *Newspapers.com.*

from Doylestown reported that she had seen the boys hitchhiking, carrying a dead racoon around North Lawrence, where she had picked them up and dropped them off on Route 30.

Detective Webb from the Akron Police Department suggested that the Norton Police check out a home in Loyal Oak that was purchased by, as he said, a "fag." The house was searched twice, and the owner was very cooperative. Another gay man became a suspect, but nothing came of it.

Empty homes, under bridges, even a lead to Nimisila Lake, a part of the Portage Lakes, came in. The police were sworn to check all leads, and as usual, this one came up short. So did a lead into Copley, where a couple called about four gunshots fired in their woods. Then a report of the boys being seen in Barberton at the Zayre's Department store came in. A clerk stood by her story that she saw both boys in the store. A stock clerk from the local Kroger's grocery store near the Zayre's store also recalled seeing the boys there.

All the while, the temperatures in the area were freezing. Akron Canton Airport reported that starting on February 18 through February 20, the temps went from a low of ten degrees to a high of seventeen degrees.

The paper bin at the Trinity Lutheran Church had been searched over and over, and the trash bin was emptied at the local Lawson's store, showing no evidence of the missing boys.

It wasn't until February 23 that the mystery of where the boys were was solved. Around 5:00 a.m., a driver for Packaging Corporation of America in Akron found the boys in the paper bin from the Lutheran church parking lot when he unloaded it. He was walking by it when he saw a swim fin sticking out from the papers. He went in search of the other and found a boot attached to one of the boys.

The bin was a hefty, semi-sized trailer, which measured seven and a half feet wide by eight feet high and was twenty-five feet long. How could the search for the boys not turn up anything when so many had checked the bin? An interview with one of Holcomb's friends revealed that lots of kids played in the bin and made forts toward the closed back end, digging down to the bottom of the bin. The paper bundles were way over their heads.

Many folks who had been seen dropping off papers at the particular bin were interviewed. One local resident said that he had stacked papers in the bin on February 17, a day before the boys went missing. He said that he stacked papers ten to fifteen feet from the closed back end of the bin, almost to the top. He stated that he came the next day and found papers had been torn down and looked different from the previous day. He also said that he got up on top of the stack and there was a hole or gully about five to ten feet back from the closed end of the bin but said that he saw nothing unusual and began filling it up the gully with bundles of papers. Another resident of Copley was interviewed by the Norton Police Department and stated that he had stacked papers in the bin on February 21 and felt that the boys may have been in the bin and checked it out.

On February 19, another Norton resident checked the bin after hearing the news of the missing boys. She stated that the bin was about half full but sloped so that she had to restack some of the papers. She mentioned that the bin floor was slippery and icy and the stacks were over her head as she went inside. Church members at Trinity Lutheran reported that the papers were always being torn down and restacked.

When the bodies were discovered, they were about fifteen feet apart and were in the rear of the trailer. Akron Police and Norton Police officers and detectives were called to the scene along with the Summit County coroner. Care was taken to diagram and photograph the scene and keep papers that were near the boys as evidence in case of foul play. Both boys were then wrapped carefully and respectfully in white sheets to prevent any debris from falling from their outer garments. The Akron Police Department, on visual inspection, said there appeared to be no signs of violence, weapons or foreign material located to have caused their deaths. The coroner took the bodies to Akron City Hospital, where they were pronounced dead by Dr. J. Andreozzi. From there, they were transported to the morgue for an autopsy. Norton Police were present during the autopsy, where again, there was no evidence of foul play, and the preliminary examination concluded that the boys died of accidental exposure. Erich still had food in his stomach, which meant that he had died four to six hours after he ate his last meal.

According to the plant manager at the packaging plant, James L. Burnworth, the box at Trinity Church was there year-round. The box that the boys were found in had been placed there on February 9 and could not be opened from the inside if the doors were closed. Several of the drivers that were questioned at the plant said that Trinity always left the doors open, and interviews with citizens assured the police that the doors were open all of the time and were never seen closed.

On March 28, 1979, according to the *Akron Beacon Journal*, during a news conference, Coroner Kyriakides of Summit County stated, "It was cold enough that it reduced the boys' body temperatures to the point where their hearts stopped beating. As they struggled, they rapidly lost energy and body heat. There was evidence of a tremendous struggle on the part of both boys to free themselves from the trailer."

He said it was possible they were trapped under as much as five feet of scrap paper. There was scrap paper found in the sleeves of the boys and under their fingernails. The final autopsy report for both boys was ventricular fibrillation from hypothermia due to entrapment in freezing ambient temperatures. It was ruled as an accident. The coroner's final ruling was that there was no evidence of foul play or of violence perpetrated on the boys by another person. They were caught beneath piles of papers and struggled unsuccessfully to escape all the while being exposed to temperatures below freezing.

On February 24, a reporter from the *Akron Beacon Journal* interviewed Charles Holcomb, the father of Mark Holcomb, who said that he had checked the paper bin and his son was not there. He said that when he was there the papers were stacked about four feet high at the closed end of the container. He said that he did not dig into the pile but walked into the container. He said that "even if the boys were at the bottom of the deepest pile, I think they could have pushed and wriggled and shimmied and gotten out of there." His wife, Barbara, was quoted as saying, "There was foul play. I don't care if they found any marks on him [Mark] or not."

A man from Clinton who was trained by the army to handle bloodhounds and other dogs that track said it would be all but impossible for the dog used by the authorities to pass the bin and not notice if the boys were there. The owner of the bloodhound used by authorities refused to answer any questions or give his name.

By June 1979, questions still swirled in the community, and the Holcomb family had time to access many more of the facts in the case and put together some of the discrepancies. They did not believe the coroner's ruling, nor were they pleased with how the case was handle by the Norton Police.

The chief investigator for the coroner's office told the parents that the ruling was to be that the boys died of asphyxiation and that drugs and alcohol and exposure had been ruled out. The day after this conversation, the coroner's ruling was exposure.

The police chief told the families that all of the available officers were in on the case, but after inquiries, many of them said they were never notified. The chief also refused three times to use the Akron Police Department bloodhound, saying it was useless. The Norton Police Department was accused of not following up on leads or showing disinterest in the case at times.

The packaging plant and the coroner's chief investigator said it was an accident, but police and packing employees said the boys were found under very little paper, which makes it implausible that they were trapped at all.

The Holcombs always believed that foul play was involved. As quoted in the *Norton Pride* on April 4, 1979, Mrs. Holcomb said, "If it was due to exposure, it must have happened somewhere other than in that bin. The bin was checked so many times during the search that someone must have put the boys in there later in the week."

The final comment in a letter to the editor of the *Akron Beacon Journal* from Mr. and Mrs. Holcomb stated, "All the family, relatives, and friends ask of the coroner and the Norton chief is that an investigation be conducted so that we may know how our child died and that justice may be carried out in this case."

The plaintiff was J. Deibel and the defendants were A. Rousch, a butcher, and P. Yoder of Loyal Oak. In an 1881 trial, Richard Knecht, also of Loyal Oak, testified on behalf of the defendants, which annoyed the plaintiff. The case concerned the acquisition of cattle and was decided in favor of Rousch and Yoder.

At 3:00 a.m., a loud banging was heard at the door of the Loyal Oak House, a hotel and tavern owned and occupied by Mr. P. Lerch and Mr. Knecht and his family. The Knechts were in charge of the hotel side of the business. Mr. Lerch came to the door to see the faces of Mr. Deibel, Mr.

The Loyal Oak House. *The Biery House and Museum, Norton.*

Meech and Mr. Stotler. The men walked into the barroom and requested breakfast. Mr. Lerch called Mr. Knecht but said it was questionable that their request would be met. As Knecht came to the room, Deible threw a heavy object at him, which missed. The weight was thrown with such power that it crashed through a wall. Had it hit its intended target, it is likely he would not have survived. Then Deible punched Knecht, who fended off the blow. The punch enlarged the existing hole as he swung and missed Knecht. Knecht defended himself and looked behind the bar for a weapon. By this time, Deible had heaved a spittoon at Knecht's head and missed again. Knecht was able to knock Deibel down and told Meech and Stotler to take him out of the place. Knecht left the bar and grabbed a hefty chair and waited in the hallway for the return of Deibel. Deible had followed Knecht, but his friends held him back. Why the attack? Deibel stated that Knecht had sworn falsely during the trial.

During the fall of 1971, Michael Neitz, eleven, made his way down to Maco Drive from his home on Neitz Drive, where he would watch the excavation and creation of a fish hatchery. He was fascinated by the machinery and the process taking place. At about one o'clock in the afternoon on October 18, 1971, his mom, Mayme Neitz, had taken him his lunch. When she could

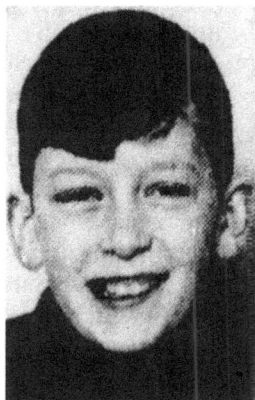

Left: Michael L. Neitz. Akron Beacon Journal, *Newspapers.com*.

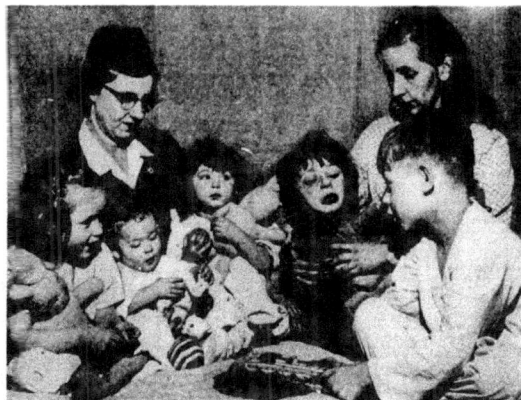

Right: Jean McConnell (*right*) and her children, who were helped by the county health department. Akron Beacon Journal, *Newspapers.com*.

not find the boy, she called the local police, who later found the body under about four feet of dirt. Apparently, Neitz had been playing behind a mound of earth when the bulldozer driver unknowingly covered the boy.

Seizures, shock, liver failure, respiratory distress, heart attack, internal bleeding, coma and sudden death are all symptoms of ingesting rat poison. Having found a tube of phosphoric poison that accidentally fell to the floor, Mary Joanne Terrion, two and a half, had consumed the toxic concoction. Mr. and Mrs. John Terrion from Norton Center rushed their daughter to the local hospital, where she was treated with an antidote and sent home. Little Mary Joanne died around midnight that same night in March 1933.

It took three Summit County welfare agencies to rescue a family of seven. Jean McConnell, twenty-nine, had a son and five daughters to tend to. The youngest, an eleven-week-old girl named Vivian was in the hospital due to malnutrition and weakness. The other four children living in dreadful conditions were Marlene, one; Barbara, three; Kathleen, five; Sandra, six; and Ronald, seven.

Thanks to a caring nurse visiting with the family, Mae Jean Gilger found that the family was crowded together and living in pitiful conditions in an old farmhouse with another family.

As the story unfolded, in 1955, the McConnells were previously living in Medina County with relatives, where they were burned out of their home. They later moved to a home in River Styx, Medina County, but fell behind on their rent. Later, the family moved to Norton Township. The transfer to Norton was for Jean and the children although, Harold McConnell was working in Norton Center at the time. That is where the child welfare services were notified of the condition of the family.

The family was later moved to the Children's Home. The welfare department did some finagling and, along with Judge Thomas, landed train tickets out of Cleveland to send the family back to their original home in Watertown, New York.

This family, in need of protection, with neglected children, serious health issues and living in squalor, finally made it to New York, where they were met by a waiting doctor.

John F. Seiberling, inventor and industrialist and father to the famed Frank A. and Charles W. Seiberling of Goodyear and Seiberling rubber fame, got notice of an accident that occurred in Norton Township. His brother, Columbus Seiberling (1848–1917), lost his left forearm when it was ground up in a horse-powered cornstalk cutting machine in 1882. Seiberling had his arm amputated a few inches below the elbow joint, and he recovered at his home near Western Star.

Clinging to life and suffering with excruciating pain, Richard Francis, six, of Western Star learned a hard lesson in 1886. A traction engine drawing a threshing machine and a water tank came through the hamlet, and a few adventurous boys wanted to hitch a ride. While swinging himself from one of the poles of the machine, Francis lost his hold and fell to the ground under the wheels of the rolling machine, where the boy was completely crushed. He died of his injuries.

FROM THE *SUMMIT COUNTY Beacon* in 1890: "His wife and children had been somewhat prepared for the terrible shock, but it came to them in the height of the Christmas festivity with a shock that almost deprived the fond wife of her reason. The children, deprived so early of all that is meant by 'father,' clung sobbing to her skirts, and to the few spectators it was a scene more terribly pitiful than that which occurred at the moment of the wreck."

This scene played out all over the area of New Portage, Akron, Barberton and Norton in 1890, when a tornado ripped through the small hamlet and canal town. Just before Christmas day on December 24, the Creedmore Cartridge Company was basically leveled while all the workmen were on the job. The story was reported to the *Akron Beacon Journal* by J.J. Orr of Norton

Center, who was a carpenter's laborer and was facing the main building when the twister hit. About a dozen carpenters were laboring all over the building putting up rafters in one part and getting ready to secure the roof. The building had three stories.

It had been extremely windy the entire day, and some of the workmen decided it was too dangerous to stay on the roof and headed down to lower levels. Some of the men decided to stay. At about 3:30 p.m., the workers heard a roaring sound like that of a freight train, some describing it as a rumbling crash. It was too late by the time they turned to look, as the funnel hit right in the center of the structure. The entire structure blew apart and collapsed along with the toiling victims. What was left was a pile of brick, rafters and mangled bodies. There was a scene of panic as the screaming of the victims was heard while they could not escape being crushed under piles of construction materials.

John Triplett was trapped beneath an enormous beam that lay across his crushed skull with the back of his scalp torn, the area wet with his blood from the cuts in his head and his neck broken

Within feet of Triplett were five others, all bruised and cut. "They were carried, a mass of blood-stained bodies and shattered limbs and laid beside their silent companion," in the words of the *Akron Beacon Journal*.

The list of injuries was as follows: John Baker, who had been hit in the head with a brick, was unconscious; B. Frank Stuver had a crushed chest, and it was consider potentially fatal; Louis Navel had a broken left leg with injuries to his spine and back; Isaiah Lower was bruised in the abdomen, back and head; Frank Mallory had a dislocated left shoulder; and I.F. Homer was injured internally and had a back injury. One of the workers said that he had been caught up in the swirling funnel that twirled him around, but he was not injured.

The Creedmore Cartridge Company was set to open in February 1890 with great anticipated fanfare in the community. It was to be one of the biggest ammunition companies in the country. Its president was the famed O.C. Barber, vice president was C.E. Sheldon and manager was W.P. Leach. Orders had already poured in from foreign countries, including Japan and Australia and parts of South America.

The building was to have and engine room, annealing and molding, priming, mixing, loading and cutting houses, as well as a warehouse.

With the intention to rebuild, W.P. Leach said that replacement of the building would cost approximately $4,000, and another 150,000 bricks would need to be acquired.

A LOOSE VICIOUS DOG pawed open swivel locks and clawed away at boards and got into the pens of show rabbits, killing fifteen of the helpless creatures. The attack occurred in 1974 in the dark of night at the home of Mr. and Mrs. Harold Krahl of Wadsworth Road. Thirteen of the dead rabbits were large New Zealand whites and the other two were Black Satins. The Krahls owned seventy rabbits, and this attack and the carnage broke a thirty-year breeding strain.

The Summit County deputy dog warden, C.A. Schmittle, said it was probably a large-breed dog by looking at the tracks in the snow, although smaller dogs do kill. He blamed the owners of the dog.

Mr. Krahl said that the owner of the dog would know it was theirs one day. He had placed a muskrat trap at the opening of the pen, assuming that the dog would be back. The dog did come back and got his paw trapped but took the trap with him attached to his paw and lived for a few more days of hunting.

THE SETTLEMENT OF $350,000 in a wrongful death suit was one of the largest awards negotiated by a jury in 1974. The suit blamed negligence by General Tire, Mogadore Chemical Plant. On November 13, 1974, Michael Linkowski, thirty-two, of Oval Drive in Norton was on a catwalk at the plant over a thirty-thousand-gallon liquid latex container when an explosion happened. The blast was so intense that it hurtled Linkowski clear over another building, where he fell thirty feet below and landed on a paved surface.

Linkowski had been a pipe fitter for twelve years and worked for Mitchell Piping Incorporated of Akron. There was some confusion about whether Linkowski had been welding at the time, which could have sparked the blast. A spokesperson for Mitchell Piping said that he was not welding at the time of the eruption because Linkowski had been waiting for a material delivery and his torches had not even been lit. Also injured in the blast was Jerry Doan, thirty-five, of Atwater; Earl Getz, twenty-three, of Canal Fulton; and John C. Schuster of Cuyahoga Falls. The blast disintegrated the tank and crumpled a nearby structure. A local resident said that he saw scrap fly at least four hundred feet in the air.

In December, it was theorized that a vapor buildup was the cause of the explosion. The Ohio Industrial Commission superintendent, Gary Bryer, said in his opinion the blast was not caused by an outside flame or spark. The blast could have happened because of peroxides building up in a holding tank. The peroxide came from butadiene, which is a gas used in the making

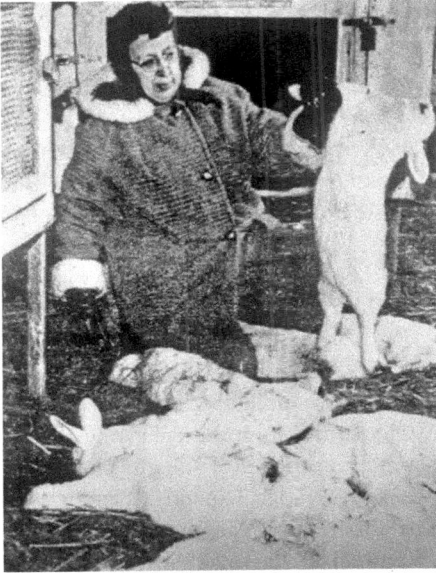

Left: Mrs. Harold Krahl shows some of her dead rabbits killed by a roaming dog. *Norton Pride*.

Right: Michael Linkowski. *Akron Beacon Journal, Newspapers.com*.

of latex. The OIC (Ohio Industrial Commission) and OSHA (Occupational Safety and Health Administration) both investigated the blast and could not come to a determination about a cause. An outside consultant and General Tire also held investigations. By January 1975, General Tire came to the conclusion that an external flame or spark set off the explosion, which disagreed with the finding of governmental studies.

Because butadiene becomes flammable as it mixes with air at certain levels, some of the reports concluded that it was a buildup of vapors and not static electricity or any activity of Michael Linkowski. General Tire made adjustments to its manufacturing of latex by changing the degassing procedures and only using those particular tanks that blew up for storage.

Michael Linkowski left behind a widow, Diane, thirty-two, and three children Ricky, six; Michael, eight; and Michelle, eleven. A heartfelt obituary in the *Norton Pride* in part read like this: "To say that a construction worker was killed when a chemical tank exploded is not enough. Mike was a devoted husband and father. He was a big busy man who enjoyed life and had a big heart."

DENNIS COLLIER, NINETEEN, PLEADED guilty to two sexual imposition charges and trespassing and was found guilty by Summit County Common Pleas judge Frank J. Bayer in 1974. Bayer later dropped the burglary and concealed weapons charge hanging over Collier's head, and Collier was released on parole in 1977 after serving part of a previous sentence at the Mansfield Reformatory on charges of rape and felonious assault. But Collier wasn't done yet. After his release, he went on to rape a seventeen-year-old Cuyahoga Falls girl while she was walking in the Sand Run Park in Akron in May 1974. He cut off most of her hair and chased down another girl who managed to escape with a mild hair cutting. Then the next month, Collier, while out free on a $10,000 bond, assaulted a thirteen-year-old girl at an Akron hotel swimming pool. As the girl ran to avoid Collier, she fell into the pool and began to struggle to swim. Collier offered her a hand up, which gave him the opportunity to do the snipping deed. He used a lengthy pair of scissors and cut off numerous inches of the girl's hair.

Finally, a new charge by Municipal Court judge Donald McFadden set bond at $20,000, while Assistant City Prosecutor William Michaels called Collier a danger to society. Known as the "Hair Snipper," in 1979, Dennis Collier, now twenty-four, was sentenced to four to ten years for posing as a doctor named Dr. Phillips. Collier somehow managed to get through security and was not noticed as he performed pelvic examinations on women who were patients at St. Thomas Hospital in Akron. Collier entered hospital rooms, performed the exams and was charged with burglary for taking locks of hair from his victims. He was also charged with concealing a weapon for bringing the scissors that he used with him to cut the women's hair. The charges were concealed weapon, criminal trespass, gross sexual imposition and aggravated burglary.

ESTATE TROUBLES CAUSED A fifty-seven-year-old farmer to take his own life in 1896. Found hanging in his barn by son Harvey, Allen P. Fritz was said to be recently antisocial and sad. The body was found hanging with a rope that had been thrown across the main beam in the center of the barn. Underneath the corpse was found a box that was used by Fritz to stand on and kick out from under his body, allowing him to freely swing until he either suffocated or broke his neck.

The Fritz farm still stands on the south side of Wadsworth Road just east of Medina Line.

Barn where Allen P. Fritz was found hanging. *Author photograph.*

In 1901, amid speculation among his friends that Joseph Rice was demoralized over the outlook of his crops and the fact that he was poor, Rice took his own life by pressing the muzzle of a revolver against his forehead and pulling the trigger. Rice, forty-two, had just moved his wife and small child into the Diehm farm just south of Loyal Oak

A skull crushed, a broken neck, an entangled mass of flesh and bone was all that was left of Dobbin in 1907. J.H. Sell of Loyal Oak shared the sad tale of Dobbin, who had lost his teammate weeks before. He was said to love another who did not return his affections. Dobbin was the loyal carriage horse for Sell and decided to end it all one fateful day in July by jumping from the upper floors of his barn.

Considering himself a nuisance on his own farm, Loyal Oak resident John J. Warner, sixty-eight, was found in his orchard having blown his entire head from his torso with a shotgun in 1923

Starting his journey in Norton Center in 1939 and following his estranged wife who took off out of Akron led to tragedy for Paul B. Breen. Following his wife to Lubbock, Texas, Breen was in search of his five-year-old son, whom he wanted sole custody of. When his wife refused, Breen swallowed poison in her presence and died a quick death. Breen had only one survivor, a sister in Kenmore.

CATHERINE O'CONNOR, THIRTY-SIX, OF Loyal Oak sued her husband, John J. O'Connor, for divorce on May 17, 1950. By May 23, 1950, John O'Connor was dead. Finding a handwritten note, O'Connor's son James was to notify his grandpa of his dad's intent. Grandpa came to the house and discovered his son dead in his still-running vehicle inside his garage.

John O'Connor had succumbed to carbon monoxide fumes, and the death was ruled a suicide by Coroner C.I. Martin.

LIVING IN A TROUBLED condition, trying to run her income tax accounting business and dealing with the death of her husband, Nellie Durham, sixty-nine, of Wadsworth Road had had enough.

Three shots were fired from a .22-caliber small-arm—two bullets into Durham's eighteen-year-old cat, Tommy, and one to her own right temple. Both bodies were found on newspapers in the basement of her home. Durham had requested nonchalantly over the phone to neighbors that they might want to stop by around 6:00 p.m., when the bodies were discovered.

AN OBITUARY IN THE *Norton Pride* in 1974 read like this: "In a deserted field 200 yards from his home, tragedy waited patiently September 27 for Joe Roudebush to return from a special football game at Norton."

What led this young man's feet into this field silently with a loaded shotgun? What frustrations over the years piled higher and higher? What resentments did he store quietly away festering? What despair burned his mind and blinded his reasoning? Were his threats of self-destruction really a cry for help? And no one heard? Was the fatal shot self-inflicted or an accident of rage? At this point, even the Norton Police cannot make a judgment.

All these questions go unanswered because Joe would be the only one who would know. "Desperation" made the threats. Was it "despair" that pulled the trigger?

Joseph Roudebush passed away on September 27 of a gunshot wound from a 20-gauge shotgun. The Summit County coroner investigated. Joe Roudebush was a fifteen-year-old living on Shellhart Road. Joe's dad found his body around 2:30 p.m. after searching all night

A FORMER NORTON MAN, Terry C. Minton, twenty-five, died in Daytona Beach Florida on August 4, 1975. The Daytona Police said that Minton died from a drug overdose. Minton had worked for Babcock and Wilcox when he lived on Symphony Lane in Norton and was a Vietnam War veteran.

The *Norton Pride* published this obituary:

Who can we blame for the death of Terry Minton by drug poisoning? What sense does it all make to those who love him most and spoke with him only a few short weeks ago? Can we blame the crowd he ran with while he was growing up at Norton? No, "needy" Hague [Teagle], Pat Morris [Shea], Dave and Dan Cook could always be found together, baling hay or riding horses, enjoying each other's families, frolicking and growing up as happy as jaybirds always together. It's so hard to believe. Returning from the service he found us all married and life styles had changed. He really just wanted to get married and have a family too.

Can we blame then his family? No. His family was very close and his little sister Shelly was devoted to her big brother and his mother and dad had only love and concern for their son.

Let's blame the school then. No, he graduated with flying colors in 1968 and hadn't even heard of drugs yet.

Let's blame the service then that took him at the prime of his youth and caused him to lose track of his friends…maybe.

Somewhere, sometime unknown to anyone but Terry and God, Terry made a decision to "try" something.

So who is left to blame? Maybe you and I for letting it happen, for hiding our heads and not seeing?

After having allegedly hit and killed a pedestrian, suspected driver Daniel Rivers, thirty-eight, took off in his plane the following day from Akron-Fulton Airport without a flight plan. In December 1996, during his final minutes while flying a single-engine airplane into Pennsylvania's Shenango Reservoir, air traffic controllers said that they heard Rivers say that he was going swimming that night.

Rivers was flying a Cessna 182-E airplane from the J-5 Flying Club in Akron, where he was a member. He was flying higher than twenty-one thousand feet, which requires pressurization or onboard oxygen. The plane was destined to run out of fuel quickly. While flying near Youngstown, Ohio, he ignored controllers as the aircraft plunged into the frozen reservoir near Sharon, Pennsylvania, killing Rivers. Being told where to land, Rivers insisted it be in water, suggesting to controllers that he was not having a good day. Rivers was a former air force sergeant and an experienced pilot.

Investigators were concerned that this was a suicide in response to the earlier hit-and-run that ultimately killed thirty-five-year-old Perry Lemley while he was walking along a Norton roadway.

Rescue workers found the plane the next day. The plane had plunged through six inches of ice and was completely submerged. After examination, the NTSB (National Transportation Safety Board) determined that the plane was not pressurized, and no oxygen tank was found inside the plane. An autopsy showed that Rivers had a blood alcohol level that was not enough to be legally drunk, at 0.04 percent, although a friend said that Rivers never drank prior to this incident

YELLING, "YOU'VE MESSED UP my life long enough," a drunk Robert Dale Morris, thirty-eight, shot his father with a .12-gauge shotgun. Morris lived with his parents on Barber Road. His mom and dad were shocked on Christmas Eve in 1961 when their son came home at 10:00 p.m. and caught them off guard with his rantings. The shotgun blast penetrated the shoulder of Robert C. Morris, sixty-one. While he was trying to reload, Morris's mother tried to intervene by grabbing the gun and wrestling it from her son. The father said for his wife to leave as he fell to the floor, where the younger Morris began beating and kicking his father.

Morris ran to the home of the next-door neighbors, Dorothy Hooser her son William Hooser, nineteen; and mother-in-law Edna Hooser. He continued his fury. "I've already shot my father; I may have to shoot you too. I've got another gun in my pocket." These words were recorded in the *Akron Beacon Journal*. Morris forced William Hooser to drive him to a Wooster Road restaurant, where Hooser called for the police. Police picked up Morris while he complained to officers about his parents, accusing them of causing his divorce and for all of his life's ills.

Morris's life was not one of roses as the police had the unemployed laborer in their sites. Morris had been charged nineteen times since 1946 for various activities, including felonious assault, driving while inebriated, assault and battery and nonsupport for minor children.

LAURI LEE LEBARRE, a sixth grader at Grill School, was killed when she was shot through the left eye by a .45-caliber revolver. On September 11, 1973, Lebarre and her sixteen-year-old cousin, Michael Patrick McQuillen, were playing around with the gun at her grandparents' home in Akron. Lebarre had asked to see the gun, which was lying on the bed in the upstairs bedroom. McQuillen had opened the cylinder, assuming the gun was unloaded, his finger slipped, and the gun fired the lethal shot.

LOYAL OAK LAKE PARK was the place to be on a hot summer day. Dug in the 1930s and opened as a swim club in 1955, the lake on Hametown Road boasted three docks with multiple diving boards and three slides. The largest slide was forty feet high with metal steps, a handrail and a wooden platform. When reaching the platform, which was surrounded by a rail, you could look over the whole park. Looking down the slide itself, you would see a metal slide with a slight bit of water coming in on the left side to wet the slide for easier transit.

For a youngster, it was a thrill to reach the top and plunge down to the water below, but it was also a bit harrowing to white knuckle it up the ladder.

The circumstances are unknown, but, seventeen-year-old Howard Huff fell forty feet, which equals one quarter of a football field, off the slide, suffering head and neck injuries on June 11, 1959. He had just graduated from Archbishop Hoban High School in Akron. Dorotha McKee, the mother of Huff, sued the park for $40,000 in common pleas court.

The slide wasn't removed from the park until 1986.

WHO WAS LIMON BROWN, whose body lies at the Western Star Cemetery? He died by being crushed by a lock stone at the age of twenty-seven. The Erie Canal was being built in this community in 1825. Perhaps he was one of the many workers to lose his life for the cause.

Limon Brown headstone in Western Star Cemetery. *Author photograph.*

6

STICK 'EM UPS

S tick 'em up!" A shower of bullets and a couple of thieves running from a looting in Barberton was the name of the game in 1931. The seriousness of the situation was certainly lost on twelve-year-old Adrian Morgan, who was along for the fun and excitement of a new crime career perpetuated by his twenty-seven-year-old brother, Lester.

The *Akron Beacon Journal* reported when asked, "Weren't you afraid when the shots came?" Adrian responded, "Afraid? What of?" He answered with a sneer of disgust. "Did your brother prevail on you to go along because you wanted to skip school?" "Naw," said the boy promptly, "I went because I wanted to."

Lester Morgan didn't invite his little brother when his partner in crime, George Worrell, twenty-eight; his wife, Edith Worrell; and Meda Chapman, twenty-nine, who was the wife of Morgan, were taken into custody. The team of outlaws were partners in a few different daylight heists. They were involved in a dozen robberies in the area.

A REAL GAME OF cops and robbers took place in Copley and ended up in Loyal Oak in 1932. Fifty shots fired and ten miles traversed at 3:00 a.m., patrolmen Harry Kimerer and George Binkley were trying to make a traffic stop. George White, thirty, and Delmar Noyes had other ideas and fled in their roadster. As White and Noyes took off, the officers fired shots in the air, trying to persuade the two men to stop. When the men would not stop, the officers began shooting at the car's tires. Three of the tires were shot out and flew off the car. The retreating men then ran the car on its rims, throwing sparks along the way and creating a noisy racket. Going through Loyal Oak, the police continued to shoot at the car. The police car almost crashed many times as they pulled up next to the fleeing vehicle. The officers finally rammed the car, and the two men lost control and struck a tree in a farmyard. White and Noyes took off on foot, and Kimerer caught one of the bandits and Binkley the other after firing more shots in the air. After arresting the men, the officers found two loaded revolvers that had been tossed into the barnyard along with a burlap sack of burglar tools in their car.

WILLIAM JONES

LEO TOPE

William Jones and Leo Tope.
Akron Beacon Journal,
Newspapers.com.

THREE NORTON MEN AND one Barberton man were charged with "uttering false stamps as true stamps" or in other words, bootlegging tax stamps in 1935. William Jones, thirty-one; Leo Tope, twenty-eight; and Russell Ott, twenty-four, of Johnson's Corners, along with Tom Stillman, forty, of Barberton stole approximately 250,000 to 1,000,000 printed sales tax stamps from the Superior Printing and Lithographing Company in Akron.

The top brass in the company said that they had been lax in preventing individuals from stealing. Guards were in attendance at the facility but admit that Jones, who worked on the cutting machine, might have been pilfering stamps here and there for quite some time. The stamps that were stolen were flawed, called "culls." They were destined to be destroyed, according to the deputy tax collector, Joseph, A. Cleary. Topes sold the stolen stamps to Ott and Stillman, who were each charged with complicity in the fraudulent use of stamps.

The state finance director, M. Ray Allison, claimed that the Superior Company was negligent.

The four men were arrested and arraigned in the Barberton Municipal Court in October 1935. Jones was ordered to spend six months in jail while Stillman and Ott were both fined twenty-five dollars. Tope had his citizenship forfeited by Judge Hunsicker and was fined for costs and put on two years of probation. Also in the order was for Tope to pay $100 to the county blind pension fund. The following month, Ott was arrested again for issuing false sales tax stamps.

STARTING A LIFE OF crime at age seventeen, Stanley Galehouse of Hametown was arrested in 1935 on burglary charges for breaking into a tavern called the Old Stone Jail just down the road from his home. This night of crime garnered him the nickname that would stick with him throughout his entire crooked career. While breaking into the tavern, unbeknownst to Galehouse, there was a night watchman who saw Galehouse and took a shot at him, hitting him in the left chin, which created a scar that ran down his neck. Hence became his crooked name, Stanley "Scarface" Galehouse. Later, it was reported in the local news that Galehouse was in cahoots with a gang of men, among them, a neighbor, Adrian Swisher, who broke into a safe at the South Akron Savings and Loan Company.

By the time 1937 rolled around, Stanley "Scarface" Galehouse was at it again, this time charged along with three other men for holdups in Akron, Wadsworth and Barberton. The gig was up when the seventeen-year-old girlfriend of Galehouse was overheard in a phone conversation stating that the wanted man with the scar sounded just like her beau and that he had flashed a roll of hundreds at her. She wanted desperately to get her picture on the front-page news. Using this information and Galehouse's name, raids took place, and the hoodlums were captured and arrested but not without some difficulty.

The gang consisted of four men, including Galehouse; Swisher, thirty-five; Eli Sich, twenty-one, of Warwick; and Harlow Goule, thirty-two, of Barberton. The young girl was arrested, and when Galehouse was confronted,

Gangsters Sich, Swisher, Gould and Galehouse. Akron Beacon Journal, *Newspapers.com.*

he ran while his mother pleaded with the detectives not to shoot her son, who was carrying an automatic weapon. Galehouse was detained with no shots fired. Later that evening, Sich was arrested in a raid on his home, as well as Swisher and finally Goule.

The crooked ring admitted to Akron detectives and deputy sheriffs to having committed at least ten crimes, including kidnapping and robbery and a list of others that follows: auto stolen in Wadsworth used in a robbery and the car abandoned, theft of auto license plates and robbery of a gas station on Route 5 north of Orville, Abe H. Mirmans Market on West Waterloo Road, William Wellock's Roadhouse on Manchester Road and a Massillon gas station.

The young girl was released from juvenile detention by order of the assistant county prosecutor, George Farr. All four bandits were arraigned, and bond was set for $20,000 each by Judge G.L. Patterson.

Galehouse was headed to Mansfield Reformatory with little chance of a pardon for at least thirteen years, but it was possible that he could come up for parole in three years. The original sentence was for ten to twenty-five years consecutively, with parole eligibility in six years. Adrian Swisher went to the Ohio State Penitentiary for ten to twenty-five years, and Goule also got ten to twenty-five.

A HOARD OF GANGSTERS' weapons was confiscated in Norton Center in 1933. Albert Moon, thirty-two, was arrested after a raid on his home. There, detectives found three hundred rounds of ammunition hidden under windowsills and floors. Also found were three submachine guns, six automatic pistols that were all loaded and $2,000 in cash. It was determined that all of the weapons had been stolen months earlier from the National Guard Armory in Barberton.

Moon had taken part in bank robberies as the driver in heists that took place in Lodi and Seville. Holdups took place in four banks in Ohio and Marleville, Pennsylvania. Six men in the ring had been arrested as of December 8, 1932, with a seventh still on the loose. The Medina grand jury indicted Moon and one of his accomplices, Walter Shoup, twenty-eight, separately on the Seville bank robbery and together with the Lodi bank robbery.

In 1933, there was a plan to spring Shoup and Moon from the Medina County Jail and then rob a Barberton bank before fleeing back to their hangout in Oklahoma. Charles "Pretty Boy Floyd" and his mob were expected to arrive, at the Kulczum farm near Copley. One member of the local mob was arrested and questioned in Wadsworth by Police Chief Tom Lucas. The youth who was questioned admitted to the plan and gave up the names of Frank Kelly, Frank Callahan and Frank Barns. The juvenile was being questioned for a gasoline station holdup and fessed up to the plot. While the boy was further questioned by the Barberton authorities, Sheriff Potts believed the young man's story, and ten Akron police, eight Barberton officers and eight deputies drove up close to the Kulczum farm. There, Potts led the men through muck and rain to sneak up on the farmhouse. With guns drawn and the word given, they rushed the house only to find Andrew Kulczum Jr., seventeen, frighteningly startled and sitting up in bed. Young Kulczum was taken to Barberton police headquarters for interrogation. He denied knowing anything about the plot.

Akron police theorized that Floyd, who had been arrested in Akron along with Frankie Mitchell when patrolman Harland Manes was killed, were indeed connected to Moon and Shoup. The jailbreak bank robbery story bears out because Floyd was in the area and the connection with Moon and Shoup. The gig was up.

BUMBLING BANDITS HIT THE Brenners Market on Cleveland Massillon road in December 1954. Four holdup men in work clothing and black masks, each with a gun, came into the market around 8:55 p.m., which was right before the store closed. There were five employees and one customer in the market, and all were forced to lie face down on the floor. One of the bandits warned that he would shoot. One of the men rustled through the cash register while the others did a pickpocket job on their victims. Off they went with their ill-gotten gain with a few cartons of cigarettes to boot only to realize that the cash they had gotten was less than the checks. They finally realized that the checks had already been cashed.

As the holdup men were leaving, lo and behold, their car would not start. In a panicked state, one of the men stole the keys of W.F. Lyon, who had just come in the store. The bandit stole Lyon's car in the parking lot and used it to shove their car that had died to get it started. Both cars proceeded on their getaway, leaving one of their companions behind waving and screaming. After realizing they were down one man, the two cars returned to the area and picked up their buddy. The stolen car was recovered in Doylestown.

One of the holdup men was described as heavy set and short, another as short and slight; one was blond and short and wore a blue sweater. No one commented on the fourth man.

By the end of December, more information poured on the four when a routine questioning of three county jail prisoners brought about the arrest of a Canton man thought to be part of the ring. The four were believed to have been involved in at least eleven burglaries in Akron and one holdup. A fifth man was being hunted. One of the three prisoners finally admitted to being part of the holdup at Brenners Market and to break-ins at bars, service stations and hardware stores. He ratted out the others.

SOURCES

Akron Beacon Journal
Akron City Times
Akron Police Department records
Cincinnati Enquirer
City of Cincinnati (website). Cincinnati.com.
"Crimes We Can't Forget." Facebook page.
Daily Leader (Lexington, Kentucky)
Daily Record (Columbus, Ohio)
Daily Times (New Philadelphia, Ohio)
Greenville Journal
Independent. IndeOnline.com.
Kentucky Advocate (Danville, Kentucky)
Lancaster Eagle-Gazette (Lancaster, Ohio)
Marysville Journal-Tribune (Marysville, Ohio)
News-Messenger (Fremont, Ohio)
Newspapers.com
Norton Police Department records
Ohio Death Penalty News-Messenger
Summit County Beacon
Summit County Medical Examiners Office, Chief Investigator, Gary Guenther
Taylor, Phyllis. *100 Years of Magic: The Story of Barberton, Ohio 1891–1991*. Akron, OH: Summit County Historical Press, 1991.
———. *Talk of the Town*. Akron, OH: Summit County Historical Press, 1996.

ABOUT THE AUTHOR

Lisa Ann Merrick has previously published a book on the history of Norton, Ohio, through Arcadia Publishing. She grew up in the Norton community and still resides there today. She enjoys sleuthing for stories for her local paper with an emphasis on history, current events and interesting individuals. She currently has three children's books that she is working on and hopes to see them published and enjoyed by children and adults alike.

Ms. Merrick has always had a fascination with the odd and interesting, crime stories, prisons, forensic and mortuary science. For this reason, she was led to research and write about murder and mayhem in her own community.

She holds an associate degree from the University of Akron, Wayne campus with an emphasis on natural science. Her joys in life include reenacting early American life, canoeing, fishing, arrowhead hunting, landscaping, stringed instruments and volunteering at her local historical society and museum. She has also been a full-time artist for the past twenty-six years, pressing and preserving flowers from their natural state.